OΩ

A BOOK OF DARTMOOR

YES TOR

A BOOK OF
DARTMOOR

S. BARING-GOULD

First published by Methuen & Co 1900
Second edition 1907
Third facsimile edition 2002

ISBN 1 84114 164 X

British Library Cataloguing-in-Publication Data
A CIP record for this title is available from the British Library

HALSGROVE
Halsgrove House
Lower Moor Way
Tiverton, Devon EX16 6SS
T: 01884 243242
F: 01884 243325
sales@halsgrove.com
www.halsgrove.com

Printed and bound in Great Britain by
Bookcraft Ltd, Midsomer Norton

TO THE MEMORY OF
MY UNCLE

THE LATE

THOMAS GEORGE BOND

ONE OF THE PIONEERS OF
DARTMOOR EXPLORATION

PREFACE

AT the request of my publishers I have written *A Book of Dartmoor:* I had already dealt with this upland district in two chapters in my *Book of the West,* vol. i., "Devon." But in their opinion this wild and wondrous region deserved more particular treatment than I had been able to accord to it in the limited space at my disposal in the above-mentioned book.

I have now entered with some fulness, but by no means exhaustively, into the subject; and for those who desire a closer acquaintance with, and a more precise guide to the several points of interest on "the moor," I would indicate three works that have preceded this.

1. Mr. J. Brooking Rowe in 1896 republished the *Perambulation of Dartmoor,* first issued by his great-uncle, Mr. Samuel Rowe, in 1848.

The original work was written by a man whose mind was steeped in the crude archæological theories of his period. The new editor could not dispense with this matter, which pervaded the work, without a complete recasting of the book, and this he was reluctant to attempt. He limited himself to cautioning the reader to put no trust in these exploded theories. The result is that the reader is tripping over uncertain ground, never knowing what is to be accepted and what rejected.

2. Mr. J. H. W. Page's *Exploration of Dartmoor*, 1889, is admirable as a guide. The author, however, was unhappily ignorant of prehistoric archæology, and allowed himself to be led astray by the false antiquarianism that had marked the early writers. Consequently, his book is capital as a guide to what is to be seen, but eminently unreliable in its explanation of the character and age of the antiquities.

3. A capital 'book is Mr. W. Crossing's *Amid Devonia's Alps*, 1888, which is wholly free from pseudo-antiquarianism. It is brief, it is small and cheap, and an admirable handbook for pedestrians.

In no way do I desire to supersede these works. I have taken pains rather to supplement them than to step into the places occupied by their writers.

The plan I have adopted in this gossiping volume is to give a general idea of the moor and of its antiquities—the latter as interpreted by up-to-date archæologists—and then to suggest rambles made from certain stations on the fringe, or in the heart of the region.

Here and there it has been inevitable that I should twice mention the same object of interest, once in the introductory portion, and again when I have to refer to it as coming within the radius of a proposed ramble.

As a boy I had an uncle, T. G. Bond, who lived near Moreton Hampstead, and who was passionately devoted to Dartmoor. He inspired me with the same love. In 1848 he presented me, as a birthday present, with Rowe's *Perambulation of Dartmoor.* It arrested my attention, engaged my imagination, and was to me almost as a Bible. When I obtained a holiday from my books, I mounted my pony and made for the moor. I rode over it, round it, put up at little inns, talked with the moormen, listened to their tales and songs in the evenings, and during the day sketched and planned the relics that I then fondly supposed were Druidical.

The child is father to the man. Years have rolled away. I have wandered over Europe, have rambled to Iceland, climbed the Alps, been for some years lodged among the marshes of Essex—yet nothing that I have seen has quenched in me the longing after the fresh air, and love of the wild scenery of

Dartmoor. There is far finer mountain scenery elsewhere, but there can be no more bracing air, and the lone upland region possesses a something of its own —a charm hard to describe, but very real—which engages for once and for ever the affections of those who have made its acquaintance. " After all said," observed my uncle to me one day, when my father had dilated on the glories of the Pyrenees, " Dartmoor is to itself, and to me—a passion." And to his memory I dedicate this volume.

My grateful thanks are due to Messrs. R. Burnard, P. F. S. Amery, J. Shortridge, and C. E. Robinson for permission to employ photographs taken by them.

S. BARING-GOULD

Lew Trenchard, Devon

CONTENTS

ILLUSTRATIONS

FULL-PAGE

ILLUSTRATIONS

DARTMOOR

CHAPTER I.

BOGS

DARTMOOR proper consists of that upland
region of granite, rising to nearly 2,000 feet
above the sea, and actually shooting above that
height at a few points, which is the nursery of many
of the rivers of Devon.

The Exe, indeed, has its source in Exmoor, and it
disdains to receive any affluents from Dartmoor; and
the Torridge takes its rise hard by the sea at Well-
combe, within a rifleshot of the Bristol Channel,
nevertheless it makes a graceful sweep — tenders a
salute — to Dartmoor, and in return receives the
liberal flow of the Okement. The Otter and the
Axe, being in the far east of the county, rise in the
range of hills that form the natural frontier between
Devon and Somerset.

B

But all the other considerable streams look back upon Dartmoor as their mother.

And what a mother! She sends them forth limpid and pure, full of laughter and leap, of flash and brawl. She does not discharge them laden with brown mud, as the Exe, nor turned like the waters of Egypt to blood, as the Creedy.

A prudent mother, she feeds them regularly, and with considerable deliberation. Her vast bogs act as sponges, absorbing the winter rains, and only leisurely and prudently does she administer the hoarded supply, so that the rivers never run dry in the hottest and most rainless summers.

Of bogs there are two sorts, the great parental peat deposits that cover the highland, where not too steep for them to lie, and the swamps in the bottoms formed by the oozings from the hills that have been arrested from instant discharge into the rivers by the growth of moss and water-weeds, or are checked by belts of gravel and boulder. To see the former, a visit should be made to Cranmere Pool, or to Cut Hill, or Fox Tor Mire. To get into the latter a stroll of ten minutes up a river-bank will suffice.

The existence of the great parent bogs is due either to the fact that beneath them lies the impervious granite, as a floor, somewhat concave, or to the whole rolling upland being covered, as with a quilt, with equally impervious china-clay, the fine deposit of feldspar washed from the granite in the course of ages.

In the depths of the moor the peat may be seen

riven like floes of ice, and the rifts are sometimes twelve to fourteen feet deep, cut through black vegetable matter, the product of decay of plants through countless generations. If the bottom be sufficiently denuded it is seen to be white and smooth as a girl's shoulder—the kaolin that underlies all.

On the hillsides, and in the bottoms, quaking-bogs may be lighted upon or tumbled into. To light upon them is easy enough, to get out of one if tumbled into is a difficult matter. They are happily small, and can be at once recognised by the vivid green pillow of moss that overlies them. This pillow is sufficiently close in texture and buoyant to support a man's weight, but it has a mischievous habit of thinning around the edge, and if the water be stepped into where this fringe is, it is quite possible for the inexperienced to go under, and be enabled at his leisure to investigate the lower surface of the covering *duvet* of porous moss. Whether he will be able to give to the world the benefit of his observations may be open to question.

The thing to be done by anyone who gets into such a bog is to spread his arms out—this will prevent his sinking—and if he cannot struggle out, to wait, cooling his toes in bog water, till assistance comes. It is a difficult matter to extricate horses when they flounder in, as is not infrequently the case in hunting; every plunge sends the poor beasts in deeper.

One afternoon, in the year 1851, I was in the Walkham valley above Merrivale Bridge digging into what at the time I fondly believed was a tumulus, but which I subsequently discovered to be a mound thrown up for the accommodation of rabbits, when a warren was contemplated on the slope of Mis Tor.

Towards evening I was startled to see a most extraordinary object approach me—a man in a draggled, dingy, and disconsolate condition, hardly able to crawl along. When he came up to me he burst into tears, and it was some time before I could get his story from him. He was a tailor of Plymouth, who had left his home to attend the funeral of a cousin at Sampford Spiney or Walkhampton, I forget which. At that time there was no railway between Tavistock and Launceston; communication was by coach.

When the tailor, on the coach, reached Roborough Down, "'Ere you are!" said the driver. "You go along there, and you can't miss it!" indicating a direction with his whip.

So the tailor, in his glossy black suit, and with his box-hat set jauntily on his head, descended from the coach, leaped into the road, his umbrella, also black, under his arm, and with a composed countenance started along the road that had been pointed out.

Where and how he missed his way he could not explain, nor can I guess, but instead of finding himself at the house of mourning, and partaking there of cake and gin, and dropping a sympathetic tear, he got up on to Dartmoor, and got—with considerable dexterity—away from all roads.

He wandered on and on, becoming hungry, feeling the gloss go out of his new black suit, and raws develop upon his top-hat as it got knocked against rocks in some of his falls.

Night set in, and, as Homer says, "all the paths were darkened"—but where the tailor found himself there were no paths to become obscured. He lay in a bog for some time, unable to extricate himself. He lost his umbrella, and finally lost his hat. His imagination conjured up frightful objects; if he did not lose his courage, it was because, as a tailor, he had none to lose.

He told me incredible tales of the large, glaring-eyed monsters that had stared at him as he lay in the bog. They were probably sheep, but as nine tailors fled when a snail put out its horns, no wonder that this solitary member of the profession was scared at a sheep.

The poor wretch had eaten nothing since the morning of the preceding day. Happily I had half a Cornish pasty with me, and I gave it him. He fell on it ravenously.

Then I showed him the way to the little inn at Merrivale Bridge, and advised him to hire a trap there and get back to Plymouth as quickly as might be.

"I solemnly swear to you, sir," said he, "nothing will ever induce me to set foot on Dartmoor again. If I chance to see it from the Hoe, sir, I'll avert my eyes. How can people think to come here for pleasure—for pleasure, sir! But there, Chinamen eat birds'-nests. There are depraved appetites among human beings, and only unwholesome-minded individuals can love Dartmoor."

There is a story told of one of the nastiest of mires on Dartmoor, that of Aune Head. A mire, by the way, is a peculiarly watery bog, that lies at the head of a river. It is its cradle, and a bog is distributed indiscriminately anywhere.

A mire cannot always be traversed in safety; much depends on the season. After a dry summer it is possible to tread where it would be death in winter or after a dropping summer.

A man is said to have been making his way through Aune Mire when he came on a top-hat reposing, brim downwards, on the sedge. He gave it a kick, whereupon a voice called out from beneath, "What be you a-doin' to my 'at?" The man replied, "Be there now a chap under'n?" "Ees, I reckon," was the reply, "and a hoss under me likewise."

There is a track through Aune Head Mire that can be taken with safety by one who knows it.

Fox Tor Mire once bore a very bad name. The only convict who really got away from Princetown and was not recaptured was last seen taking a bee-line for Fox Tor Mire. The grappling irons at the disposal of the prison authorities were insufficient for the search of the whole marshy tract. Since the mines were started at Whiteworks much has been done to drain Fox Tor Mire, and to render it safe for grazing cattle on and about it.

There is a nasty little mire at the head of Redaven Lake, between West Mill Tor and Yes Tor, and there is a choice collection of them, inviting the unwary to their chill embraces, on Cater's Beam, about the sources of the Plym and Blacklane Brook, the ugliest of all occupying a pan and having no visible outlet. The Redlake mires are also disposed to be nasty in a wet season, and should be avoided at all times. Anyone having a fancy to study the mires and explore them for bog plants will find an elegant selection around Wild Tor, to be reached by ascending Taw Marsh and mounting Steeperton Tor, behind which he will find what he desires.

"On the high tableland," says Mr. William Collier, "above the slopes, even higher than many tors, are the great bogs, the sources of the rivers. The great northern bog is a vast tract of very high land, nothing but bog and sedge, with ravines down which the feeders of the rivers pour. Here may be found Cranmere Pool, which is now no pool at all, but just a small piece of bare black bog. Writers of Dartmoor guide-books have been pleased to make much of this Cranmere Pool, greatly to the advantage of the living guides, who take tourists there to stare at a small bit of black bog, and leave their cards in a receptacle provided for them. The large bog itself is of interest as the source of many rivers; but there is absolutely no interest in Cranmere Pool, which is nothing but a delusion and a snare for tourists. It was a small pool years ago, where the rain water lodged; but at Okement Head hard by a fox was run to ground, a terrier was put in, and by digging out the terrier Cranmere Pool was tapped, and has never been a pool since. So much for Cranmere Pool!

"This great northern bog, divided into two sections by Fur Tor and Fur Tor Cut, extends southwards to within a short distance of Great Mis Tor, and is a vast receptacle of rain, which it safely holds throughout the driest summer.

Fur Tor Cut is a passage between the north and south parts of this great bog, evidently cut artificially for a pass for cattle and men on horseback from Tay Head, or Tavy Head, to East Dart Head, forming a pass from west to east over the very wildest part of Dartmoor. Anyone can walk over the bogs ; there is no danger or difficulty to a man on foot unless he gets exhausted, as some have done. But horses, bullocks, and sheep cannot cross them. A man on horseback must take care where he goes, and this Fur Tor Cut is for his accommodation."*

The Fur Tor Mire is not composed of black but of a horrible yellow slime. There is no peat in it, and to cross it one must leap from one tuft of coarse grass to another. The "mires" are formed in basins of the granite, which were originally lakes or tarns, and into which no streams fall bringing down detritus. They are slowly and surely filling with vegetable matter, water-weeds that rot and sink, and as this vegetable matter accumulates it contracts the area of the water surface. In the rear of the long sedge grass or bogbean creeps the heather, and a completely choked-up mire eventuates in a peat bog. Granite has a tendency to form saucer-like depressions. In the Bairischer Wald, the range dividing Bavaria from Bohemia, are a number of picturesque tarns, that look as though they occupied the craters of extinct volcanoes. This, however, is not the case ; the rock is granite, but in this case the lakes are so deep that they have not as yet been filled with

---

* "Dartmoor," in the *Transactions of the Plymouth Institution*, 1897-8.

vegetable deposit. On the Cornish moors is Dosmare Pool. This is a genuine instance of the lake in a granitic district. In Redmoor, near Fox Tor, on the same moors, we have a similar saucer, with a granitic lip, over which it discharges its superfluous water, but it is already so much choked with vegetable growth as to have become a mire. Ten thousand years hence it will be a great peat bog.

I had an adventure in Redmoor, and came nearer looking into the world beyond than has happened to me before or since. Although it occurred on the Cornish moors, it might have chanced on Dartmoor, in one of its mires, for the character of both is the same, and I was engaged in the same autumn on both sets of moors. Having been dissatisfied with the Ordnance maps of the Devon and Cornish moors, and desiring that certain omissions should be corrected, I appealed to Sir Charles Wilson, of the Survey, and he very readily sent me one of his staff, Mr. Thomas, to go over the ground with me, and fill in the particulars that deserved to be added. This was in 1891. The summer had been one of excessive rain, and the bogs were swollen to bursting. Mr. Thomas and I had been engaged, on November 5th, about Trewartha Marsh, and as the day closed in we started for the inhabited land and our lodgings at " Five Janes." But in the rapidly closing day we went out of our course, and when nearly dark found ourselves completely astray, and worst of all in a bog. We were forced to separate, and make our way as best we could, leaping from one patch of rushes or moss to another. All at once I went in over my waist, and felt myself being sucked down as though an octopus had hold of me. I cried out, but Thomas could neither see me nor assist me had he been able to approach. Providentially I had a long bamboo, like an alpenstock, in my hand, and I laid this horizontally on the surface and struggled to raise myself by it. After some time, and with desperate effort, I got myself over the bamboo, and was finally able to crawl away like a lizard on my face. My watch was stopped in my waistcoat pocket, one of my gaiters torn off by the suction of the bog, and I found that for a moment I had been submerged even over one shoulder, as it was wet, and the moss clung to it.

On another occasion I went with two of my children, on a day when clouds were sweeping across the moor, over Langstone Moor. I was going to the collection of hut circles opposite Greenaball, on the shoulder of Mis Tor. Unhappily, we got into the bog at the head of Peter Tavy Brook. This is by no means a dangerous morass, but after a rainy season it is a nasty one to cross.

Simultaneously down on us came the fog, dense as cotton wool. For quite half an hour we were entangled in this absurdly insignificant bog. In getting about in a mire, the only thing to be done is to leap from one spot to another where there seems to be sufficient growth of water-plants and moss to stay one up. In doing this one loses all idea of direction, and we were, I have no doubt, forming figures of eight in our endeavours to extricate ourselves. I knew that the morass was inconsiderable in extent, and that by taking a straight line it would be easy to get out of it, but in a fog it was not possible to take a bee-line. Happily, for a moment the curtain of mist lifted, and I saw on the horizon, standing up boldly, the stones of the great circle that is planted on the crest. I at once shouted to the children to follow me, and in two minutes we were on solid land.

The Dartmoor bogs may be explored for rare plants and mosses. The buckbean will be found and recognised by its three succulent sea-green leaflets, and by its delicately beautiful white flower tinged with pink, in June and July. I found it in 1861 in abundance in Iceland, where it is called *Alptar colavr*, the swan's clapper. About Hamburg it is known as the "flower of liberty," and grows only within the domains of the old Hanseatic Republic. In Iceland it serves a double purpose. Its thickly interwoven roots are cut and employed in square pieces like turf or felt as a protection for the backs of horses that are laden with packs. Moreover, in crossing a bog, the clever native ponies always know that they can tread safely where they see the white flower stand aloft.

The golden asphodel is common, and remarkably lovely, with its shades of yellow from the deep-tinted buds to the paler expanded flower. The sundew is everywhere that water lodges; the sweet gale has foliage of a pale yellowish green sprinkled over with dots, which are resinous glands. The berries also are sprinkled with the same glands.

The plant has a powerful, but fresh and pleasant, odour, which insects dislike. Country people were wont to use sprigs of it, like lavender, to put with their linen, and to hang boughs above their beds. The catkins yield a quantity of wax. The sweet gale was formerly much more abundant, and was largely employed; it went by the name of the Devonshire myrtle. When boiled, the wax rises to the surface of the water. Tapers were made of it, and were so fragrant while burning, that they were employed in sick-rooms. In Prussia, at one time, they were constantly furnished for the royal household.

The marsh helleborine, *Epipactis palustris*, may be gathered, and the pyramidal orchis, and butterfly and frog orchises, occasionally.

The furze—only out of bloom when Love is out of tune—keeps away from the standing water. It is the furze which is the glory of the moor, with its dazzling gold and its honey breath, fighting for existence against the farmer who fires it every year, and envelops Dartmoor in a cloud of smoke from March to June. Why should he do this instead of employing the young shoots as fodder?

I think that as Scotland has the thistle, Ireland the shamrock, and Wales the leek as their emblems, we Western men of Devon and Cornwall should adopt the furze. If we want a day, there is that of our apostle S. Petrock, on June 4th.

By the streams and rivers and on hedgebanks the yellow broom blazes, yet it cannot rival in intensity of colour and in variety of tint the magnificent furze

or gorse. But the latter is not a pleasant plant to
walk amidst, owing to its prickles, and especial care
must be observed lest it affix one of these in the
knee. The spike rapidly works inwards and pro-
duces intense pain and lameness. The moment it
is felt to be there, the thing to be done is immediately
to extract it with a knife. From the blossoms of
the furze the bees derive their aromatic honey,
which makes that of Dartmoor supreme. Yet bee-
keeping is a difficulty there, owing to the gales, that
sweep the busy insects away, so that they fail to
find their direction home. Only in sheltered combes
can they be kept.

The much-relished Swiss honey is a manufactured
product of glycerine and pear-juice; but Dartmoor
honey is the sublimated essence of ambrosial sweetness in taste and savour, drawn from no other source
than the chalices of the golden furze, and com-
pounded with no adventitious matter.

CHAPTER II.

TORS

SEEN from a distance, as for instance from
Winkleigh churchyard, or from Exbourne, Dartmoor presents a stately appearance, as a ridge of
blue mountains rising boldly against the sky out of
rolling, richly wooded underland.

But it is only from the north and north-west that it
shows so well. From south and east it has less
dignity of aspect, as the middle distance is made
up of hills, as also because the heights of the
encircling tors are not so considerable, nor is their
outline so bold.

Indeed, the southern edge of Dartmoor is conspicuously tame. It has no abrupt and rugged
heights, no chasms cleft and yawning in the range,
such as those of the Okement and the Tavy and Taw.
And to the east much high ground is found rising in
stages to the fringe of the heather-clothed tors.

Dartmoor, consisting mainly of a great upheaved
mass of granite, and of a margin of strata that have

A TOR, SHOWING WEATHERING OF GRANITE

been tilted up round it, forms an elevated region some thirty-two miles from north to south and twenty from east to west.   The heated granite has altered the slates in contact with it, and is itself broken through on the west side by an upward gush of molten matter which has formed Whit Tor and Brent Tor.

The greatest elevations are reached on the out-skirts, and there, also, is the finest scenery.   The interior consists of rolling upland.   It has been likened to a sea after a storm suddenly arrested and turned to stone ; but a still better resemblance, if not so romantic, is that of a dust-sheet thrown over the dining-room chairs, the backs of which resemble the tors divided from one another by easy sweeps of turf.

Most of the heights are crowned with masses of rock standing up like old castles ; these, and these only, are tors.*   Such are the worn-down stumps of vast masses of mountain formation that have dis-appeared.   There are no lakes on or about the moor, but this was not always so.   Where is now Bovey Heathfield was once a noble sheet of water fifty fathoms deep.   Here have been found beds of lignite, forests that have been overwhelmed by the wash from the moor, a canoe rudely hollowed out of an oak, and a curious wooden idol was exhumed leaning against a trunk of tree that had been swallowed up in a freshet.   The canoe was nine feet long.   Bronze spear-heads have also been found in this ancient lake, and moulds for casting bronze instruments.   A

---

* The Welsh *twr* is a tower ; *twrr*, a heap or pile. From the same root as the Latin *turris*.

representation of the idol was given in the *Trans-actions of the Devonshire Association* for 1875.

The new Plymouth Reservoir overlies an old lake-bed. Taw Marsh was also once a sheet of rippling blue water, but the detritus brought down in the weathering of what once were real mountains has filled them all up. Dartmoor at present bears the same relation to Dartmoor in the far past that the gums of an old hag bear to the pearly range she wore when a fresh girl. The granite of Dartmoor was not well stirred before it was turned out, consequently it is not homogeneous. Granite is made up of many materials : hornblende, feldspar, quartz, mica, schorl, etc. Sometimes we find white mica, some-times black. Some granite is red, as at Trowles-worthy, and the beautiful band that crosses the Tavy at the Cleave ; sometimes pink, as at Leather Tor ; sometimes greenish, as above Okery Bridge ; some-times pure white, as at Mill Tor.

The granite is of very various consistency, and this has given it an appearance on the tors as if it were a sedimentary rock laid in beds. But this is its little joke to impose on the ignorant. The feature is due to the unequal hardness of the rock which causes it to weather in strata.

The fine-grained granite that occurs in dykes is called elvan, which, if easiest to work, is most liable to decay. In Cornwall the elvan of Pentewan was used for the fine church of S. Austell, and as a consequence the weather has gnawed it away, and the greater part has had to be renewed. On the other hand, the splendid elvan of Haute Vienne has supplied the cathedral of Limoges with a fine-grained material that has been carved like lace, and lasts well.

The drift that swept over the land would appear to have been from west to east, with a trend to the south, as no granite has been transported, except in the river-beds to the north or west, whereas blocks have been conveyed eastward. This is in accordance with what is shown by the long ridges of clay on the west of Dartmoor, formed of the rubbing down of the slaty rocks that lie north and north-west. These bands all run north and south on the sides of hills, and in draining processes they have to be pierced from east to west. This indicates that at some period during the Glacial Age there was a wash of water from the north-west over Devon, depositing clay and transporting granite.

On the sides of the tors are what are locally termed "clitters" or "clatters" (Welsh *clechr*), consisting of a vast quantity of stone strewn in streams from the tors, spreading out fanlike on the slopes. These are the wreckage of the tor when far higher than it is now, *i.e.* of the harder portions that have not been dissolved and swept away.

"The tors—Nature's towers—are huge masses of granite on the top of the hills, which are not high enough to be called mountains, piled one upon another in Nature's own fantastic way. There may be a tor, or a group of tors, crowning an eminence, but the effect, either near or afar, is to give the hilltop a grand and imposing look. These large blocks of granite, poised on one another, some appearing as if they must fall, others piled with curious regularity—considering they are Nature's work—are the

C

prominent features in a Dartmoor landscape, and, wild as
parts of Dartmoor are, the tors add a notable picturesque
effect to the scene.   There are very fine tors on the western
side of the moor.   Those on the east and south are not so
fine as those on the north and west.   In the centre of the
moor there are also fine tors.   They are, in fact, very numerous, for nearly every little hill has its granite cap, which is
a tor, and every tor has its name.   Some of the high hills
that are torless are called beacons, and were doubtless used
as signal beacons in times gone by.   As the tors are not
grouped or built with any design by Nature to attract the
eye of man, they are the more attractive on that account,
and one of their consequent peculiarities is that from different points of view they never appear the same.   There can
be no sameness in a landscape of tors when every tor
changes its features according to the point of view from
which you look at it.   Every tor also has its heap of rock
at its feet, some of them very striking jumbles of blocks of
granite scattered in great confusion between the tor and the
foot of the hill.   Fur Tor, which is in the very wildest spot
on Dartmoor, and is one of the leading tors, has a *clitter* of
rocks on its western side as remarkable as the tor itself ;
Mis Tor, also on its western side, has a very fine clitter
of granite ; Leather Tor stands on the top of a mass of
granite rocks on its east and south sides ; and Hen Tor, on
the south quarter, is surrounded with blocks of granite, with
a hollow like the crater of a volcano, as if they had been
thrown up by a great convulsion of Nature.   Hen Tor is
remarkable chiefly for this wonderful mass of granite blocks
strewn around it.   All the moor has granite boulders
scattered about, but they accumulate at the feet of the tors
as if for their support."*

* COLLIER, *op. cit.*

VIXEN TOR

Here among the clitters, where they form caves, a search may be made for the beautiful moss *Schistostega osmundacea.* It has a metallic lustre like green gold, and on entering a dark place under rocks, the ground seems to be blazing with gold. In Germany the Fichtel Gebirge are of granite, and the Luchsen Berg is so called because there in the hollow under the rocks grew abundance of the moss glittering like the eyes of a lynx. The authorities of Alexanderbad have had to rail in the grottoes to prevent the *gold moss* from being carried off by the curious. Murray says of these retreats of the luminous moss :—

"The wonder of the place is the beautiful phosphorescence which is seen in the crannies of the rocks, and which appears and disappears according to the position of the spectator. This it is which has given rise to the fairy tales of gold and gems with which the gnomes and cobolds tantalise the poor peasants. The light resembles that of glow-worms; or, if compared to a precious stone, it is something between a chrysolite and a cat's-eye, but shining with a more metallic lustre. On picking up some of it, and bringing it to the light, nothing is found but dirt."

Professor Lloyd found that the luminous appearance was due to the presence of small crystals in the structure which reflect the light. Coleridge says :—

> "'Tis said in Summer's evening hour,
> Flashes the golden-coloured flower,
> A fair electric light."

In 1843, when the luminosity of plants was recorded in the *Proceedings of the British Association*, Mr. Babington mentioned having seen in the south of England a peculiar bright appearance produced by the presence of the *Schistostega pennata*, a little moss which inhabited caverns and dark places : but this was objected to on the ground that the plant reflected light, and did not give it off in phosphorescence.*

When lighted on, it has the appearance of a handful of emeralds or aqua marine thrown into a dark hole, and is frequently associated with the bright green liverwort. Parfitt, in his *Moss Flora of Devon*, gives it as *osmundacea*, not as *pennata*. It was first discovered in Britain by a Mr. Newberry, on the road from Zeal to South Tawton ; it is, however, to be found in a good many places, as Hound Tor, Widdecombe, Leather Tor, and in the Swincombe valley, also in a cave under Lynx Tor. If found, please to leave alone. Gathered it is invisible; the hand or knife brings away only mud.

But what all are welcome to go after is that which is abundant on every moorside—but nowhere finer than on such as have not been subjected to periodical " swaling " or burning. I refer to the whortleberry. This delicious fruit, eaten with Devonshire cream, is indeed a delicacy. A gentleman from London was visiting me one day. As he was fond of good things, I gave him whortleberry and cream. He ate it in dead silence, then leaned back in his chair,

* HARDWICKE'S *Science Gossip*, 1871, p. 123.

looked at me with eyes full of feeling, and said, " I am thankful that I have lived to this day."

The whortleberry is a good deal used in the south of France for the adulteration and colouring of claret, whole truck-loads being imported from Germany.

There is an interesting usage in my parish, and I presume the same exists in others. On one day in summer, when the "whorts" are ripe, the mothers unite to hire waggons of the farmers, or borrow them, and go forth with their little ones to the moor. They spend the day gathering the berries, and light their fires, form their camp, and have their meals together, returning late in the evening, very sunburnt, with very purple mouths, very tired maybe, but vastly happy, and with sufficient fruit to sell to pay all expenses and leave something over.

If the reader would know what minerals are found on Dartmoor he must go elsewhere.

I have a list before me that begins thus : "Allophane, actinolite, achroite, andalusite, *apatite*"— but I can copy out no more. I have often found *appetite* on Dartmoor, but have not the slightest suspicion as to what is apatite. The list winds up with wolfram, about which I can say something. Wolfram is a mineral very generally found along with tin, and that is just the "cussedness" of it, for it spoils tin.

When tin ore is melted at a good peat fire, out runs a silver streak of metal. This is brittle as glass, because of the wolfram in it. To get rid of the wolfram the whole has to be roasted, and the operation is delicate, and must have bothered our forefathers considerably. By means of this second process the wolfram, or tungsten as it is also called, is got rid of.

Now, it is a curious fact that the tin of Dartmoor is of extraordinary purity; it has little or none of this abominable wolfram associated with it, so that it is by no means improbable that the value of tin as a metal was discovered on Dartmoor, or in some as yet unknown region where it is equally unalloyed.

In Cornwall all the tin is mixed with tungsten. Now this material has been hitherto regarded as worthless; it has been sworn at by successive generations of miners since mining first began. But all at once it has leaped into importance, for it has been discovered to possess a remarkable property of hardening iron, and is now largely employed for armour-plated vessels. From being worth nothing it has risen to a rapidly rising value, as we are becoming aware that we shall have to present impenetrable sides to our Continental neighbours.

Dartmoor comprises the "forest" and the surrounding commons, as extensive together as the forest itself. "What have you got on you, little girl?" asked a good woman of a shivering child. "Please, mem, first there's a jacket, then a gownd, and then comes Oi." So with Dartmoor. First come the venville parishes, next their extensive commons, and "then comes Oi," the forest itself.

The venville parishes are all moorland parishes— Belstone, Throwleigh, Gidleigh, Chagford, North Bovey, Manaton, Widdecombe, Holne, Buckfastleigh, Dean Prior, South Brent, Shaugh, Meavy,

Sheeps Tor, Walkhampton, Sampford Spiney, Whitchurch, Peter Tavy, Lydford, Bridestowe, Sourton.
There are others, standing like the angel of the
Apocalypse, with one foot on the moorland, the
other steeped in the green waves of foliage of the
lowlands; such are South Tawton, Cornwood, and
Tavistock. Others, again, as Lustleigh, Bridford,
Moreton, Buckland-in-the-Moor, Ilsington, and Ugborough, must surely have been moorland settlements at one time, and Okehampton itself is as distinctly a moor town as is Moreton, which tells its
own tale in its name. But all these have their warm
envelope of arable land, groves and woods, farms
and hamlets. Such have their commons, over which
every householder has a right to send cattle, to take
turf and stone, and, alas! with the connivance of the
other householders, to inclose. This inclosing has
been going on at a great rate in some of the parishes.
For instance, common rights are exercised by the
householders of South Zeal over an immense tract
of land on the north side of Cosdon. Of late years
they have put their heads together and decided, as
they are few in number, to appropriate it to themselves as private property, and inclosures have proceeded at a rapid rate.

In Bridestowe there is a tract of open land on
which the poor cotters have, from time immemorial,
kept their cows. But they are tenants, and not householders, and have consequently no rights. The seven
or eight owners have combined to inclose and sell or
let for building purposes all that tract of moor, and
the cotters have lost their privilege of keeping cows.

What we see now going on under our eyes has been going on from time immemorial. Parishes have encroached, and the genuine forest has shrunk together before them. The commons still exist, and are extensive, but they are being gradually and surely reduced. "Then comes Oi!" Look at the map and see of what the forest really consists. It surely must have been larger formerly.

On the forest itself are a certain number of "ancient tenements," thirty-five in all. These are of remote antiquity. On certainly most of them, probably on all, the plough and the hoe turn up numerous flint tools, weapons, and chips—sure proof that they were settlements in prehistoric times. These tenements are at Brimpts, Hexworthy, Huccaby, Bellever, Dunnabridge, Baberry, Pizwell, Runnage, Sherberton, Riddons, Merripit, Hartland, Broom Park, Brown Berry, and Prince Hall. These were held—and some still are—by copy of the Court Roll, and the holders are bound to do suit and service at the Court. It is customary for every holder on accession to the holding to inclose a tract of a hundred acres, and this inclosure constitutes his newtake.

The forest belongs to the Prince of Wales, but I believe has never been visited by him. Were he to do so, he would be surprised, and perhaps not a little indignant, to see how his tenants are housed. A forest does not necessarily signify a wood. It is a place for wild beasts. The origin of the word is not very clear. Lindwode says, " A Forest is a place where are wild beasts ; whereas a Park is a place

ROCKS NEAR HEY TOR

where they are shut in." Ockam says, "A Forest is
a safe abode for wild beasts," and derives the word
from *feresta*, *i.e.* a place for wild creatures. It was, in
fact, a tract of uninclosed land reserved for the king
to hunt in, and a *chase* was a similar tract reserved by
the lord of the manor for his own hunting.

It is more than doubtful whether Dartmoor was
ever covered with trees. No doubt there have been
trees in the bottoms, and indeed oak has been
taken from some of the bogs; but the charcoal found
in the fire-pits of the primitive inhabitants of the
moor in the Bronze Age shows that, even in the prehistoric period, the principal wood was alder, and that
such oak as there was did not grow to a large size,
and was mainly confined to the valleys that opened
out of the moor into the lowlands. Up these, doubtless, the forest crept. Elsewhere there may have
been clusters of stunted trees, of which the only
relics are Piles and Wistman's Wood. There were
some very fine oaks at Brimpts, and also in Okehampton Park, but these were cut down during the
European war with Napoleon. After the wood at
Brimpts had fallen under the axe, it was found that
the cost of carriage would be so great that the timber
was sold for a mere trifle, only sufficient to pay for
the labour of cutting it down.

The forest is divided into four quarters, in each of
which, except the western, is a pound for stray
cattle. Formerly the Forest Reeve privately com-
municated with the venville men when he had fixed
a day for a "drift," which was always some time
about midsummer. Then early in the morning all

assembled mounted. A horn was blown through a holed stone set up on a height, and the drift began. Cattle or horses were driven to a certain point, at which stood an officer of the Duchy on a stone, and read a proclamation, after which the owners were called to claim their cattle or ponies. Venville tenants removed them without paying any fine, but all others were pounded, and their owners could not recover them without payment of a fine.

The Duchy Pound is at Dunnabridge, where is a curious old seat within the inclosure for the adjudicator of fines and costs. It is apparently a cromlech that has been removed or adapted. The Duchy now lets the quarters to the moormen, who charge a small fee for every sheep, bullock, or horse turned out on the moor not belonging to a venville man, and for this fee they accord it their protection.

A good deal of money has been expended on the reclaiming of Dartmoor. Sir Thomas Tyrwhitt, Usher of the Black Rod, was Warden of the Stannary and Steward of the Forest for George IV. when Prince of Wales. He fondly supposed that he had discovered an uncultivated land, which needed only the plough and some lime to make its virgin soil productive. He induced others to embark on the venture. Swincombe and Stannon were started to become fine farm estates. Great entrance gates were erected to where mansions were proposed to be built. But those who had leased these lands found that the draining of the bogs drained their pockets much faster than the mires, and abandoned the attempt

which had ruined them. Others followed. Prince's
Hall was rebuilt with fine farm buildings by a Mr.
Fowler from the north of England, who expended
his fortune there and left a disappointed man.
Before him Sir Francis Buller, who had bought
Prince's Hall, planted there forty thousand trees—
such as are not dead are distorted starvelings. Mr.
Bennett built Archerton, near Post Bridge, and inclosed thousands of acres. He cannot have recovered
a sum approaching his outlay in the sixty years of
his tenancy. The fact is that Dartmoor is cut out
by Nature to be a pasturage for horses, cattle, and
sheep in the summer months, and for that only.
In the burning and dry summers of 1893, 1897, and
1899 tens of thousands of cattle were sent there,
even from so far off as Kent, where water and
pasturage were scarce, and on the moor they both
are ever abundant.

Tenements there must be, but they should be
in the sheltered valleys, and the wide hillsides and
sweeps of moor should be left severely alone. As
it is, encroachments have gone on unchecked, rather
have been encouraged. Every parish in Devon has
a right to send cattle to the moor, excepting only
Barnstaple and Totnes. But the Duchy, by allowing
and favouring inclosures, is able to turn common
land into private property, and that it is only too
willing to do.

Happily there now exists a Dartmoor Preservation Society, which is ready to contest every attempt
made in this direction. But it can do very little to
protect the commons around the forest—in fact it

can do nothing, if the freeholders in the parishes that enjoy common rights agree together to appropriate the land to themselves—and for the poor labourer who is able to buy himself a cow it can do nothing at all, for his rights have no legal force.

CHAPTER III.

THE ANCIENT INHABITANTS

Abundance of remains of primeval inhabitants—No trace of Briton or
Saxon on Dartmoor—None of Palæolithic man—The Neolithic man
who occupied it—Account of his migrations—His presence in
Ireland, in China, in Algeria—A pastoral people—The pottery—
The arrival of the Celt in Britain in two waves—The Gael—The
Briton—Introduction of iron— Mode of life of the original occupants
of the moor—The huts—Pounds—Cooking—Tracklines—Enormous
numbers who lived on Dartmoor—A peaceable people.

PROBABLY no other tract of land of the same
extent in England contains such numerous and
well-preserved remains of prehistoric antiquity as
Dartmoor.

The curious feature about them is that they all
belong to one period, that of the Early Bronze, when
flint was used abundantly, but metal was known,
and bronze was costly and valued as gold is now.

Not a trace has been found so far of the peoples
who intervened between these primitive occupants
and the mediæval tin-miners.

If iron was introduced a couple of centuries before
the Christian era, how is it that the British inhabitants
who used iron and had it in abundance have left
no mark of their occupancy of Dartmoor? It can
be accounted for only on the supposition that they
did not value it. The woods had been thinned

and they preferred the lowlands, whereas in the earlier period the dense forests that clothed the country were too close a jungle and too much infested by wolves to be suitable for the habitation of a pastoral people.

That under the Roman domination the tin was worked on the moor there is no evidence to show. No Roman coins have been found there except a couple brought by French prisoners to Princetown.

It may be said that iron would corrode and disappear, whereas flint is imperishable, and bronze nearly so. But where is Roman pottery? Where is even the pottery of the Celtic period? An era is distinguished by its fictile ware. A huge gap in historic continuity is apparent. All the earthenware found on Dartmoor is either prehistoric or mediæval, probably even so late as the reign of Elizabeth.

No indication is found that the Saxons worked the tin or even drove their cattle on to the moor. In Domesday Book Dartmoor is not even mentioned. It is hard to escape the conclusion that from the close of the prehistoric period to that of our Plantagenet kings, Dartmoor was avoided as a waste, inhospitable region.

Of man in the earliest period at which he is known to have existed—the so-called Palæolithic man—not a trace has been found on Dartmoor. Probably when he lived in Britain the whole upland was clothed in snow. He has left his tools in the Brixham and Torquay caves—none in the bogs of the moor. Indeed, when these bogs have been dug into, there are not the smallest indications found of man having visited the moor before the advent of what is called the Neolithic Age.

About the man of this period I must say something, as he in his day lived in countless swarms on this elevated land. He may have lived also in the valleys of the lowlands, but his traces there have been obliterated by the plough. First of all as to his personal appearance. He was dark-haired, tall, and his head was long, like that of a new-born child, or boat-shaped, a form that disappears with civilisation, and resolves itself into the long face instead of the long head.

At some period, vastly remote, a great migration of a long-headed race took place from Central Asia. It went forth in many streams. One to the east entered Japan ; probably the Chinese and Anamese represent another. But we are mainly concerned with the western outpour. It traversed Syria, and Gilead and Moab are strewn with its remains, hut circles, dolmens, and menhirs identical with those on Dartmoor. Hence one branch passed into Arabia, where, to his astonishment, Mr. Palgrave lighted on replicas of Stonehenge.*

* " Hardly had we descended the narrow path, when we saw before us several huge stones, like enormous boulders, placed endways perpendicularly, on the soil, while some of them yet upheld similar masses, laid transversely over their summit. They were arranged in a curve once forming part, it would appear, of a large circle, and many other like fragments lay rolled on the ground at a moderate distance ; the number of those still upright was, to speak by memory, eight or nine. Two, at about ten or twelve feet apart one from the other, and resembling huge gateposts, yet bore their horizontal lintel, a long block laid across them ; a few were deprived of their upper traverse, the rest supported each its headpiece in defiance of time and the more de-

Another branch threw itself over the Himalayas, and covered India with identical monuments. Again another turned west; it traversed the Caspian and left innumerable traces along the northern slopes of the Caucasus. The Kuban valley is crowded with their dolmens. They occupied the Crimea, and then struck for the Baltic. That a branch had passed through Asia Minor and Greece, and constituted itself as the Etruscan power in Italy, is probable but not established. The northern stream strewed Mecklenburg and Hanover with its remains, occupied Denmark and Lower Sweden, crossed into Britain, and took complete possession of the British Isles. Other members of the same swarm skirted the Channel and crowded the plateaux and moors of Western and Central France with their megalithic remains. The same people occupied Spain and Portugal, the Balearic Isles, Corsica and Sardinia,

---

structive efforts of man. So nicely balanced did one of these cross-bars appear, that in hope it might prove a rocking-stone, I guided my camel right under it, and then, stretching up my riding-stick at arm's length, could just manage to touch and push it; but it did not stir. Meanwhile the respective heights of camel, rider, and stick, taken together, would place the stone in question full fifteen feet from the ground. These blocks seem, by their quality, to have been hewed from the neighbouring limestone cliffs and roughly shaped, but present no further trace of art, no groove or cavity of sacrificial import, much less anything intended for figure or ornament. The people of the country attribute their erection to the Dārim, and by his own hands too, seeing that he was a giant. Pointing towards Rass, our companions affirmed that a second and similar stone circle, also of gigantic dimensions, existed there; and, lastly, they mentioned a third towards the south-west, that is, in the direction of Henakeeyah."—PALGRAVE, *Narrative of a Year's Journey through Central Arabia*, 1865, vol. i p. 251.

and Northern Africa, and are now represented by the Koumirs and Kabyles. To this race the name of Iberian, Ivernian, or Silurian has been given. It contributed its name to Ireland (Erin or *Ierne*), where it maintained itself, but was known to the conquering Gaels as the Tuatha da Danann and Firbolgs, two branches of the same stock. The name of Damnonia given to Devon is probably due to these same Danann, who were also found in the south of Scotland. When this great people reached Europe, Japan India, Africa, before its branches had begun to ramify to east and west, to south and north, its religious doctrines and its practices had become stereotyped, and almost ineradicably ingrained into the consciousness of the entire stock.

If we desire to understand what their peculiar views were, what were the dominant ideas which directed their conduct, and which led them to erect the monuments which are marvels to us, even at the present day, we must go to China.

Let us look for a moment into China at the present day. At first sight, the Chinese strike us as being not only geographically our antipodes, but as being our opposites in every particular — mental, moral, social; in language as in ideas.

The Chinese language is without an alphabet and without a grammar. It is made up of monosyllables that acquire their significance by the position in which they are placed in a sentence. In customs the Chinese differ from us as much. In mourning they wear white; a Chinese dinner begins with the dessert and ends with the soup; a scholar, to recite

D

his lessons, turns his back on the teacher. But it is chiefly in the way in which the living and the dead are regarded as forming an indissoluble commonwealth, that the difference of ideas is most pronounced. Regard for the dead is the first obligation to a Chinese. A man of the people who is ennobled, ennobles, not his descendants, but his ancestry. The duty of the eldest son of the family is to maintain the worship of the ancestors. Denial of a sepulchre is the most awful punishment that can be inflicted ; a Chinese will cheerfully commit suicide to gain a suitable tomb and cult after death. The most sacred spot on earth is the mausoleum, and that is perpetually inviolable. Consequently, if this principle could be carried out to the letter, the earth would be transformed into one vast necropolis, from the occupation of which the living would be in time entirely excluded. It is this respect for graves which stands in the way of the execution of works of public utility, such as canals and railroads ; and it is the imperious obligation of maintaining the worship of ancestors that blocks conversion to Christianity. It is resentment against lack of respect shown to the dead, neglect of duty to the dead, which has provoked the massacres of Christians. A Chinese, under certain circumstances, is justified in strangling his father, but not in omitting to worship him after he has throttled him.

On the great Thibet plateau, geographically contiguous to the Chinese, and under the Empire of China, the Mongol nomads are so absolutely devoid of a grain of respect for their dead, that, without the smallest scruple, they leave the corpses of their parents and children on the face of the desert, to be devoured by dogs and preyed on by vultures

If we look at the Nile valley we see that the ancient Egyptians were dominated by the same ideas as the Chinese. To them the tomb was the habitation *par excellence* of the family. Of the dwelling-houses of the old Egyptians the remains are comparatively mean, but their mausoleums are palatial. The house for the living was but as a tent, to be removed; but the mansion of the dead was a dwelling-place for ever.

Not only so, but just as the ancient Egyptian supposed that the *Ka*, the soul, or one of the souls of the deceased, occupied the monument, tablet, or obelisk set up in memorial of the dead, so does the Chinese now hold that a soul, or emanation from the dead, enters into and dwells in the memorial set up, apart from the tomb, to his honour.

Now if we desire to discover what was the distinguishing motive in life of the long-headed Neolithic man, we shall find it in his respect for the dead; and he has stamped his mark everywhere where he has been by the stupendous tombs he has erected, at vast labour, out of unwrought stones. He cannot be better described than as the dolmen-builder; that is to say, the man who erected the family or tribal ossuaries that remain in such numbers wherever he has planted his foot.

In China, it is true, there are no dolmens, but for this there is a reason. Before the descendants of the Hundred Families who entered the Celestial Empire had reached and obtained possession of mountains whence stone could be quarried, many centuries elapsed, and forced the Chinese to make shift with other material than stone, and so formed their habit of entombment without stone; but the frame of mind which, in a rocky land, would have prompted them to set up dolmens remained unchanged, and so remains to the present day.

The exploration of dolmens in Europe reveals that they were family or tribal burial-places, and were used for a long continuance of time. The dead to be laid in them were occasionally brought from a distance, as the bones show indication of having been cleaned of the flesh with flint scrapers, and to have been rearranged in an irregular and unscientific manner, a left leg being sometimes applied to a right thigh; or it may be that on the anniversary of an interment the bones of the deceased were taken out, scraped and cleaned, and then replaced.

In Algeria, and on the edge of the Sahara, are found great trilithons, that is to say, two huge upright stones, with one laid across at the top, forming doorways leading to nothing, but similar to those which are found at Stonehenge.

What was this significance?

We turn to the Chinese for an explanation, and find that to this day they erect triumphal gates—not now of stone, but of wood—in memory of and in honour of such widows as commit suicide so as to join their dear departed husbands in the world of spirits. On the other hand, our widows forget us and remarry.

The dolmen-builders were people with flocks and

herds, and who cultivated grain and spun yarn.
Their characteristic implement is the so-called celt,
in reality an axe, sometimes perforated for the re-
ception of a handle, most commonly not. The
perforation belongs to the latest stage of Neolithic
civilisation. Their weapons, or tools, were first

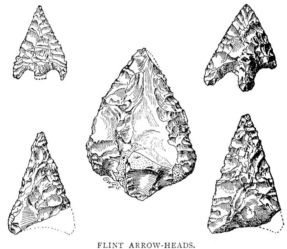

FLINT ARROW-HEADS.
(Actual size.)

ground. In about a score of places in France polishing rocks exist, marked with the furrows made by
the axe when worked to and fro upon them, and
others that are smaller have been removed to
museums. At Stoney-Kirk, in Wigtownshire, a
grinding-stone of red sandstone, considerably hollowed by use, was found with a small, unfinished
axe of Silurian schist lying upon it. In the recent

exploration of hut circles at Legis Tor a grindstone was found in one of the habitations, and on it an incomplete tool that was abandoned there before it was finished.

After grinding, these implements underwent laborious polishing by friction with the hand or with leather.

At the same time that these artificially smoothed tools were fabricated, flint was used, beautifully chipped and flaked, to form arrow and spear heads and swords. The arrow-heads are either leaf-shaped or tanged.

The pottery of the dolmen-builders is very rude. It is made of clay mingled with coarse fragments of stone or shell, is very thick and badly tempered; it is hand-made, and seems hardly capable of enduring exposure to a brisk fire. The vessels have usually broad mouths, with an overhanging rim like a turned-back glove-cuff, and below this the vessel rapidly slopes away. The ornamentation is constant everywhere. It consisted of zigzags, chevrons, depressions made by twisted cord, and finger-nail marks in rings round the bowls or rims. It was not till late in the Bronze Age that circles and spirals were adopted.

Celtic ornamentation is altogether different.

Whilst the long-headed dolmen-builder crept along the coast of Europe, there was growing up among the mountains and lakes of Central Europe a hardy round-headed race—the Aryan, destined to be his master. Was it through instinct of what was to be, that the Ivernian shrank from penetrating into the heart of the Continent, and clung to the seaboard?

When the dolmen-builder arrived in Britain, to the best of our knowledge, he found no one there. On the Continent, on the other hand, if he went far inland, he not only clashed with the Aryan round-heads, but also here and there stumbled on the lingering remains of the primeval Palæolithic people, who have left their remains in England in the river-drift, and in Devon in the Brixham caves and Kent's Hole.

The dolmen-builder has persisted in asserting himself. Though cranial modifications have taken place, the dusky skin, and the dark eyes and hair and somewhat squat build, have remained in the Western Isles, in Western Ireland, in Wales, and in Cornwall. It is still represented in Brittany. It is predominant in South-Western France, and is typical in Portugal.

After a lapse of time, of what duration we know not, a great wave of Aryans poured from the mountains of Central Europe, and, traversing Britain, occupied Ireland. This was the Gael. This people subjugated the Ivernian inhabitants, and rapidly mixed with them, imposing on them their tongue, except in South Wales, where the Silurian was found to have retained his individuality when conquered by Agricola in A.D. 78. But if the Gaelic invaders subjugated the Ivernians, they were in turn conquered by them, though in a different manner. The strongly marked religious ideas of the long-headed men, and their deeply rooted habit of worship of ancestors, impressed and captured the imagination of their masters, and as the races became fused, the mixed race continued to build dolmens and erect other megalithic monuments once characteristic of the long-heads, often on a larger scale than before. Stonehenge and Avebury were erections of the Bronze Period, and late in it, and of the composite people.

If we look at the physique of the two races, we find a great difference between them. The Ivernian was short in stature, with a face mild in expression, oval, without high cheek-bones, and without strongly characterised supraciliary ridges. The women were all conspicuously smaller than the men, and of markedly inferior development. The conquering race was other. The lower jaw was massive and square at the chin, the molar bones prominent, and the brows heavy. The head was remarkably short, and the face expressed vigour, was coarse, and the aspect threatening. Moreover, the women were as fully developed as the men, so much so that where all the bones are not present it is not always easy to distinguish the sex of a skeleton of this race. What Tacitus says of the German women—that they are almost equal to the men both in strength and in size—applies also to these round-headed invaders of Britain; and, indeed, what we are assured of the Britons in the time of Boadicea, that it was *solitum feminarum ductu bellare*, shows us that the same masculine character belonged to the women of British origin. The average difference in civilised races in the stature of men and women at present is about four inches, but twice this difference is very usually found to exist between the male and female skeletons of the Polished Stone Period in the long barrows. The difference is even more strikingly shown by a comparison of the male and female collar-bones ; and we are able to reproduce from them in picture the Neolithic woman of the Ivernian race, with narrow chest and drooping shoulders, utterly unlike the muscular and vigorous Gaelic women who were true consorts to their men when they came over to conquer the island of Britain.

After a lapse of time the long head began to re-assert itself, and the infusion of its blood into the veins of the dominant race led to great modification of its harshness of feature. When iron was introduced into Britain, whether by peaceable means or whether by the second Aryan invasion, that of the Cymri or Britons, we do not know, but when Cæsar landed in Britain, B.C. 55, he found that iron was in general use.

The second Aryan invasion alluded to was that of the true Britons. They also came from the Alps, where they had lived on platforms constructed on the lakes. They occupied the whole of Britain proper, but not Scotland, and made but attempts to effect a landing in Ireland.

They were entirely out of sympathy with the original race and its ideas, and did not assimilate their religion and adopt their practices as had the Gaels.

The distinction between the two branches of the great Celtic family is mainly linguistic. Where the British employed the letter *p*, the Gael used the hard *c*, pronounced like *k*. For instance, *Pen*, a head,

in British, is *Cen* in Gaelic; and we can roughly tell
where the population was British by noticing the
place names, such as those beginning with Pen.
When these were Gaels, the same headlands would
begin with Cen.

> " By Tre, Pol, and Pen
> You know the names of Cornishmen,"

and this at once decides that the inhabitants of the
western peninsula were not Gaels.

From the lakes of Switzerland the Britons had
brought with them their great aptitude for wattle-
work. They built their houses and halls, not of
stone, but of woven withies. Cæsar says that they
were wont to erect enormous basket-work figures,
fill them with human victims, and burn the whole as
sacrifices to their gods. It is a curious coincidence
that on some of the old Celtic crosses are found
carved imitations of men made of wicker - work.
These represent saints made of the same material
and in the same manner by the same people, after
they had embraced Christianity and abandoned
human sacrifices.*

Let us try to imagine what was the mode of life
of those people who raised their monuments on
Dartmoor. They were pastoral, but they also
certainly had some knowledge of tillage. In certain
lights, hillsides on the moor show indications of
having been cultivated in ridges, and this not with
the plough, but with the spade. We cannot say

* *Archæologia*, vol. l. Pl. 2 (1887).

that these belong to the early population, but as they are found near their settlements it is possible that they may be traces of original cultivation. But we know from the remains of grain found in the habitations and tombs of the same people in limestone districts that they were acquainted with cereals, and their grindstones have been found on Dartmoor in their huts.

Still, grain was not the main element of their diet; they lived chiefly on milk and flesh. In the huts have been found broad vessels that were covered with round discs of slate, and it is probable that these were receptacles for milk or butter, but the milk would mainly be contained in wooden or leathern vessels. Elsewhere their spindle-whorls have been found in fair abundance; not so on Dartmoor—as yet only two have been recovered. This shows that little spinning was done, and no weights such as are used by weavers have been found. The early occupants were in the main clothed in skins.

Their huts were circular, of stone, with very frequently a shelter wall, opposed to the prevailing south-west wind, screening the door, which opened invariably to the south or south-west. The whole was roofed over by poles planted on the walls, brought together in the middle, and thatched over with rushes or heather. The walls were rarely above four feet six inches high. They are lined within with large stones, set up on end, their smooth surfaces inwards, and the stone walls were backed up with turf without, making of the huts green mounds. This gave occasion to the fairy legends of the Celts, who represented the earlier population as living in mounds, which the Irish called *sidi*, and the people occupying them the Tuatha da Danann. As already said, this same name meets us in Damnonii, the oldest appellation for the people of Devon. They were a sociable people, clustering together for mutual protection in *pounds*.

These pounds are large circular inclosures, the walls probably only about four feet high, but above this was a breastwork of turf or palisading. Outside the pound were huts, perhaps of guards keeping watch.

Many of the huts have paddocks connected with them, as though these latter had been kail gardens, but some of these paddocks are large enough to have been tilled for corn. Their plough, if they used one, was no more than a crooked beam, drawn by oxen. It is possible that the numerous sharp flakes of flint that are found were employed fastened into a sort of harrow, as teeth. Their cooking was done either in pots sunk in the soil, or in holes lined with stones.

Rounded pebbles, water-worn, were amassed, and baked hot in the fire, then rolled to the "cooking-hole," in which was the meat, and layers of hot stones and meat alternated, till the hollow receptacle was full, and the whole was then covered with sods till the flesh was cooked.

The following account of the manner in which the Fiana, the Irish militia, did their cooking in pre-Christian times will illustrate this custom :—

"When they had success in hunting, it was their custom in the forenoon to send their huntsman, with what they

had killed, to a proper place, where there was plenty of
wood and water; there they kindled great fires, into which,
their way was, to throw a number of stones, where they
continued till they were red hot; then they applied themselves to dig two great pits in the earth, into one of which,
upon the bottom, they were wont to lay some of these hot

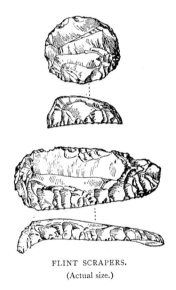

FLINT SCRAPERS.
(Actual size.)

stones as a pavement, upon them they would place the
raw flesh, bound up hard in green sedge or bulrushes;
over these bundles was fixed another layer of hot stones,
then a quantity of flesh, and this method was observed till
the pit was full. In this manner their flesh was sodden or
stewed till it was fit to eat, and then they uncovered it;
and, when the hole was emptied, they began their meal."*

* KEETING *History of Ireland* (ed. O'Connor, Dublin, 1841), i.
p. 293.

Some of the huts are very large, and in these no traces of fires and no cooking-holes have been found. Adjoining them, however, are smaller huts that are so full of charcoal and peat ash and fragments of pottery that no doubt can be entertained that these were the kitchens, and the large huts were summer habitations.

Occasionally a small hut has been found with a large hole in the centre crammed with ashes and round stones, the hole out of all proportion to the

COOKING-POT.

size of the hut if considered as a habitation. No reasonable doubt can be entertained that these were bath huts. The Lapps still employ the sweating-houses. They pour water over hot stones, and the steam makes them perspire profusely, whereupon they shampoo themselves or rub each other down with birch twigs.

Indeed, men wearing skin dresses are obliged to go through some such a process to keep their pores in healthy action.

It is very probable that the long tracklines that extend over hill and vale on Dartmoor indicate tribal boundaries, limits beyond which the cattle of one clan might not feed. Some of these lines, certainly of the age of the Neolithic men of the hut circles, may be traced for miles. There is one that starts apparently from the Plym at Trowlesworthy Warren, where are clusters of huts and inclosures. It follows the contour of the hills to Pen Beacon, where it curves around a collection of huts and strikes for the source of the Yealm by two pounds containing huts. That it went further is probable, but recent inclosures have led to its destruction. We cannot be sure of the age of these tracklines unless associated with habitations, as some very similar have been erected in recent times as reeves delimiting mining rights.

That the occupants of the moor at this remote period loved to play at games is shown by the numbers of little round pebbles, carefully selected, some for their bright colours, that have been found on the floors of their huts. That they used divination by the crystal is shown by clear quartz prisms having been discovered tolerably frequently. These are still employed among the Australian natives for seeing spirits and reading the future.

That these early people were monogamists is probable from the small size of their huts; they really could not have accommodated more than one wife and her little family.

That they were a gentle, peaceable people is also apparent from the rarity of weapons of war. Plenty of flint scrapers are found for cleaning the hides, plenty of rubber-stones for smoothing seams, plenty of small knives for cutting up meat, but hardly a spear-head, and arrow-heads are comparatively scarce. Their most formidable camp is at Whit Tor, the soil of which is littered with flint chips. It did not, on exploration, yield a single arrow-head. The pounds were inclosed to protect the sheep and young cattle against wolves, not to save the scalps of their owners from the tomahawks of their fellow-men.

With regard to the numbers of people who lived on Dartmoor in prehistoric times, it is simply amazing to reflect upon. Tens of thousands of their habitations have been destroyed; their largest and most populous settlements, where are now the "ancient tenements," have been obliterated, yet tens of thousands remain. At Post Bridge, within a radius of half a mile, are fifteen pounds. If we give an average of twenty huts to a pound, and allow for habitations scattered about, not inclosed in a pound, and give six persons to a hut, we have at once a population, within a mile, of 2,000 persons.

Take Whit Tor Camp. To man the wall it would require 500 men. Allow to each man five non-combatants; that gives a population of 2,500. There are pounds and clusters of hut circles in and about Whit Tor that still exist, and would have contained that population. Take the Erme valley, high up where difficult of access; the number of huts there crowded on the hill slopes is incredible. On the height is a cairn, surrounded by a ring of stones, from which leads a line of upright blocks for a

distance of 10,840 feet. Allow two feet apart for
the stones, that gives 5,420 stones. If, as is probable,

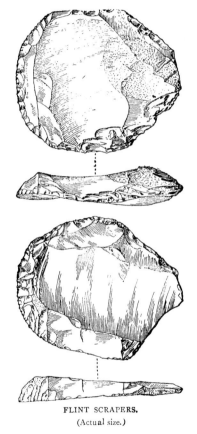

FLINT SCRAPERS.
(Actual size.)

each stone was set up by a male member of a tribe,
in honour of his chief who was interred in the cairn,
we are given by this calculation a population of over

E

21,000, allowing three children and a female to each male.

But numerous though these occupants of the moor must have been, they must have been wretchedly poor. The vast majority of their graves yield nothing but a handful of burnt ash, not a pot-

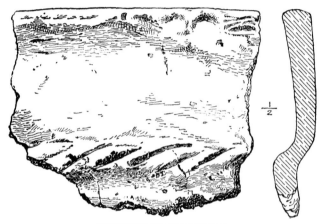

FRAGMENT OF COOKING-POT.

sherd, not a flint-chip, and the grave of a chief only a little blade of bronze as small as a modern silver pocket fruit-knife.

That they were a peaceable people I have no manner of doubt, for there are absolutely no forti-fied hilltops on the moor, which there assuredly would be were the denizens of that upland region in strife one with another. What camps there are may be found on the fringe, Whit Tor, Dewerstone, Hembury, Holne, Cranbrook, Halstock, as against invaders. That they were a happy people I cannot doubt. They were uncivilised: and the Tree of Knowledge, under high culture, bears bitter fruit for the many and drips with tears, but it bears nuts—only for the few.

CHAPTER IV.

THE ANTIQUITIES

AS already intimated, the antiquities found on Dartmoor belong almost exclusively to the Prehistoric Period. The few exceptions are the crosses and the blowing-houses. These shall be spoken of in other chapters. In this we will confine ourselves to a general review of the relics left to show how that the moor was occupied by a large population in the early Bronze Period.

Now, although these relics are very numerous, they are none of them megalithic, that is to say, very huge. And this for two reasons. In the first place it is uncertain whether the people occupying the moor ever did erect any huge stones, like the Stonehenge monsters, or the enormous dolmens of Brittany, and above all of the sandstone districts of the Loire.

In the second place, in the fifteenth and first half of the sixteenth centuries the great bulk of the churches round Dartmoor were rebuilt, and in the sixteenth and seventeenth centuries the manor houses, bartons, and farms were also reconstructed, and then for the first time since the sixth century was granite employed in ecclesiastical and domestic architecture. The builders delighted in selecting huge stones. They employed monoliths for their pillars; each door and window had a single stone on each side as a jamb, and a single stone as a base; two stones above were used for the arch of every door and window. The amount of granite of a large size carried away from the moor is really prodigious, and no large monument was likely to have been spared.

Then came the eighteenth and nineteenth centuries, when granite was in demand for gateposts, and every standing stone serviceable was ruthlessly carried away. Almost every circle of upright stones has lost some of its finest blocks in this way, and all that is left to show where they were is the hole cut in the "calm" from which they were extracted, and the *spalls* or chips made by the quarrymen as they knocked the block into shape. At Sherberton was a fine circle : the three largest stones have been employed a few yards off as gateposts, and two others have been cast down.

Next came the newtake-wall builders. The ravage they have wrought is incalculable. In 1848 S. Rowe published his *Perambulation of Dartmoor*, and gave an illustration of double stone rows that ran from the Longstone, near Caistor Rock, for half a mile to the Teign. In 1851 I planned them. A few years ago a farmer built a newtake wall, and used the rows as his quarry; nothing now is left of them but a few insignificant stones he did not consider worth his while to remove. The stones are in the wall, and can be recognised, and the socket-holes can all be traced, with a spade.

There was a row or set of rows of stones on a common near Leusden. In 1898 the road-menders destroyed it and employed the stones for the repair of the Ashburton highway.

Now it is quite possible that the old rude stone monument builders did not erect really mighty structures on Dartmoor, but it is still more likely that all such as were of any size have been carried away. Lake-head Hill, near Post Bridge, must at one time have been a veritable necropolis. The farmer at Bellever was given his holding on a rent that was to be mainly paid by inclosing newtakes, and repairing old walls. For six years he was employed in clearing Lake-head Hill of all the stones he could find. Thousands of loads were removed, and it is only by a lucky chance that one or two kistvaens have escaped. Three pounds with their huts, probably scores of kistvaens, and certainly several stone rows, have been obliterated by this man. In 1851 I drew the finest moor kistvaen at Merrivale Bridge. The covering stone measured 9 feet 3 inches by 4 feet 9 inches. In 1891 a man at Merrivale Bridge wanting a gatepost, cut one out of the capstone and left only two scraps *in situ*.

Considering the ruthless manner in which these monuments of a hoar antiquity have been carried away or destroyed, it is a marvel that any remain; but then, this devastation explains why those allowed to remain are such only as were considered too insignificant to offer inducement to the plunderer. The late Mr. Bennett, of Archerton, when inclosing and planting, utilised a fine pound for a clump of beech. The old inclosing ring was used up to make a wall for the protection of the young trees, and these latter, in growing, threw all the huts that had not been despoiled out of shape and into inextricable confusion.

Let us now take in their order such monuments as remain, and I will say a few words about each kind.

1. Of the characteristic *dolmen*, which we in England perhaps improperly call *cromlech*, we have but a single good example, that at Drewsteignton. The dolmen was the family mausoleum. It is composed of several large slabs set upright in box-form, and covered with one or more large stones, flat on the under side. These were probably all originally covered with earth, but in course of time the earth has been washed or trodden away. In some cases the dolmen becomes the *allée couverte*, a long chamber or hall constructed of uprights and coverers. The most magnificent example is that at Saumur, on the Loire, which is over 62 feet long and 13 feet wide, and high enough for a tall man to walk about in it with ease.

In these the dead were interred, not burnt, and

their bones seem to have been taken out on anniversaries, scraped, and then replaced ; and remoter ancestors were huddled into the background to make room for new-comers.

In time the fashion for carnal interment gave way to one for cremation.

Now of the large dolmen or cromlech we have only the fine Drewsteignton example, and that deserves a visit. Formerly it was but one of a number of monuments, lines and circles of upright stones. All these have been destroyed in this century.

But although this is the sole remaining example, we know by place names that anciently there were many more. These monuments have everywhere a local designation. In France they are *pierres levées* or *cabannes des fées*. In Devon they were shelf-stones, and wherever we meet with a farm called Shilston, there we may confidently assert that a dolmen formerly existed. With a little search the portions of it may occasionally be recognised in pigsties, or worked into the structure of the house.

The parish of Bradstone derives its name from the broad coverer of a cromlech, which is now employed as a stile. The supporters have disappeared, used probably for the church. There is a shilstone in Bridestowe, and another in Modbury. In dolmens it is usual to have a hole in the end stone, and even sometimes closed with a stone plug, or else a small stone is employed that could easily be removed, so as to enable those who desired it to enter and put therein food for the consumption of the dead, or to

The Pedigree of a Tomb.

Drewsteignton
Cromlech.

Merrivale Kistvaen.
—before mutilation—

Altar Tomb,
Sourton.

THE PEDIGREE OF A TOMB

remove the remains for the annual scraping, or again for the introduction of a fresh tenant.

2. When carnal interment gave way to incineration, at once the need for large mausoleums ceased, and mourners saved themselves the labour of erecting. huge cromlechs, and contented themselves instead with the more modest *kistvaen*, or stone chest. This is constructed in precisely the same manner as the dolmen, but is much smaller. A beautiful·diminutive example, from Peter Tavy Common, has been transported to the Plymouth Municipal Museum. It measures 21 inches long, 13 inches wide, and 14 inches deep. On Dartmoor there are many hundreds of these kistvaens, of various sizes, but most have been rifled by treasure-seekers ; indeed, all but such as were covered with earth and so escaped observation have been plundered.

The kistvaens were always buried under cairns, and almost invariably a circle of stones surrounded the cairn, marking its bounds.

The finest kistvaens are—one at Merrivale Bridge, one adjoining a pound near Post Bridge, one on Lake-head Hill, one near Drizzlecombe, one on Hound Tor, and two on the slope of Bellever. One is near the Powder Mills. There are several, also, about the Plym.

3. The *stone circle* is called by the French a cromlech. The name means curved stone. The circle, of which Stonehenge is the noblest known example in Europe, consists of a number of stones set up at intervals in a ring. The purport is purely conjectural. Undoubtedly interments have been made

within them; but none, so far, have been found in those on Dartmoor. In the great circle on Penmaenmawr there were burials at the foot of several of the monoliths, and, indeed, one of these served as the backstone of a kistvaen.

Among semi-barbarous tribes it is customary that the tribe should have its place of assembly and consultation, and this is marked round by either stones or posts set up in the ground. Among some of the great clan circles, if one of the constituent tribes fails to send its representative, the stone set up where he would sit is thrown down.

The areas within the circles on Dartmoor, so far as they have been examined, show that great fires have been lighted in them; the floors are thickly bedded in charcoal. It may be that they were the crematoria of the tribe, and certainly numerous cairns and kistvaens are to be found around them; or it may be that great fires were lighted in them when the tribe met for its parliament, or its games and war-dances. It has been noticed that usually these circles of upright stones are placed on the neck of land between two rivers.

Some have speculated that they were intended for astronomical observation, and for determining the solstices; but such fancies may be dismissed till we have evidence of their being erected and employed for such a purpose by some existing savage race.

The Samoyeds were wont to make circles of stones of rude blocks set up, and these are still to be seen in the ˙districts they inhabit; and although these people are nominally Christians, yet they are secretly addicted to their old paganism. Mr. Jackson, in his *Great Frozen Land* (London, 1895), says :—

"The rings of stones which I frequently met with in Waigatz are the sites of their midnight services, and are made, of course, by the Samoyeds. They are called yon-pa-ha-pai. It is possible that within these circles the human sacrifices with which Samoyeds used to propitiate Chaddi were offered up; and, although these are things of the past now, it is only a few years ago that a Samoyed, living in Novaia Zemlia, sacrificed a young girl" (p. 89).

A tradition or fancy relative to more than one of these circles is that the stones represent maidens who insisted on dancing on a Sunday, and were, for their profanity, turned into stone when the church bells rang for divine service. It is further said that on May Day or Midsummer Day they dance in a ring.

There are several of these circles on the moor. The finest are those of Scaur Hill, near Chagford, of the Grey Wethers—two side by side, but most of the stones of one are fallen — the circle on Langstone Moor above Peter Tavy, Trowlesworthy, Sherberton, and Fernworthy. The diameters vary from thirty-six feet to three hundred and sixty. One that must have been very fine was near Huccaby, but most of the stones constituting it have been removed for the construction of a wall hard by.

The number of stones employed varies according to the area inclosed.

4. The *stone row* is almost invariably associated with cairns and kistvaens, and clearly had some relation to funeral rites. The stone settings are often single, sometimes double, or are as many as eight. They do not always run parallel ; they start from a cairn, and end with a blocking-stone set across the line. In Scotland they are confined to Caithness. The finest known are at Carnac, in Brittany. It is probable that just as a Bedouin now erects a stone near a fakir's tomb as a token of respect, so each of these rude blocks was set up by a member of a tribe, or by a household, in honour of the chief buried in the cairn at the head of the row.

It is remarkable how greatly the set stones vary in size. Some are quite insignificant, and could be planted by a boy, while others require the united efforts of three, four, or even many men, with modern appliances of three legs and block, to lift and place them in position. This seems to show that the rows are not the result of concerted design, but of individual execution as the ability of the man or family permitted to set up a stone large or small. Usually the largest stones are planted near the cairn, and they dwindle to the blocking-stone, which is of respectable size.

There is no district known so rich in stone rows as Dartmoor. As many as fifty have been observed. The finest are those of Drizzlecombe, where there are three double rows, not parallel ; Down Tor, a single line ; Merrivale Bridge, two parallel double rows, but the stones constituting them small ; Stall Moor, a single line that looks like a procession of cricketers

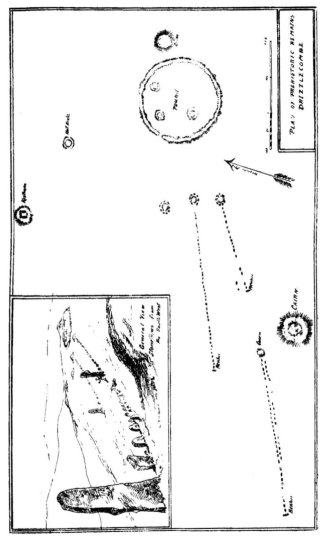

PLAN OF PREHISTORIC REMAINS
DRIZZLECOMBE

STONE-ROWS, DRIZZLECOMBE

in flannels stalking over the moor; Challacombe; at Glazebrook are thirteen rows; also Staldon Moor. Some of these rows which are small are nevertheless instructive. On the north slope of Cosdon is a cairn that originally contained three kistvaens, one of which is perfect, one exists in part, and evidence of the existence of the third was found on exploration. From this cairn start three rows of stones, one for each kistvaen. A remarkably perfect set of stone rows is on Watern Hill, behind the Warren Inn, on the road from Post Bridge to Moreton. It is actually visible from the road, but as the stones are small it does not attract attention. It starts from a cairn and a tall upright stone set at right angles to the rows, which are brought to a termination by blocking-stones. Another perfect row is at Assacombe, starting from a cairn with two or three big upright stones, and running down a rather steep hill to a blocking-stone which remains intact.

The longest of all the rows is that on Staldon, which springs from a circle of 59 feet 9 inches in diameter, inclosing the remains of a cairn, runs with a single line for two miles and a quarter, and crosses the Erme river. Had a straight line been followed, an obstruction in the precipitous bank of the river would have been encountered, to avoid which the builders of this great monument took a sweep eastward, where the bank was more sloping. In the Cosdon lines of stones already referred to, the rows waver so as to avoid a platform of rock in which the constructors were unable to plant their stones.

At Drizzlecombe there is a cairn with which is

connected a row 260 feet long, with an upright stone 17 feet 9 inches high at the end of the row.

All sorts of random guesses have been made about these rows. Some have made them out to be sacred *cursi*, where races were run, but then some lines are single, some are eightfold. Others have supposed that these were the supporting stones to cattle sheds, but these stones are often not more than 2 feet 6 inches high, and the rows often run for over 600 feet.

We must, as already said, look to present usage for their interpretation, and that afforded by the practice of the Khassias of the Brahmapootra, and by the Bedouin, seems the simplest—stones set up as memorials or tributes of respect to the dead man who is buried at the head of the row.

There would seem to have been no feeling attached to the direction in which these lines run.

One singular feature is that in several cases a second row starts off from a small cairn in or close to the main row, and runs away in quite a different direction.*

5. The *menhir*, or tall stone, is a rude, unwrought obelisk. In some cases it is nothing other than the starting or the blocking stone of a row which has been destroyed. This is the case with that at Merrivale Bridge. But such is not always the case. There were no rows in connection with the menhirs on Devil Tor and the Whitmoor Stone.

That the upright block is a memorial to the dead

* Merrivale Bridge, Har Tor, and Longstone, near Caistor Rock.

can hardly be doubted; it was continued to be erected, with an inscription on it, in Romano-British times, and its modern representative is in every churchyard.

The menhirs, locally termed longstones, or langstones, must at one time have been numerous. There was a langstone near Sourton, another by Tavistock, one at Sheeps Tor, others by Modbury; these stones have disappeared and have left but their names to tell where they once stood. One on Peter Tavy Common gave its title to the moor which the Ordnance surveyors have rendered Launceston Moor. The stone is at one end of a row, and served as a waymark over the down. It had fallen, but is re-erected.

But there are still a good many remaining. The tallest is one already referred to at Drizzlecombe. Bairdown Man (*maen* = a stone) is by Devil Tor in a singularly desolate spot. We have none comparable to the Devil's Arrows at Boroughbridge in Yorkshire—but the best have been carried away to serve as monolithic church pillars.

The Chinese hold that the spirits of the dead inhabit the memorials set up in their honour; and the carved monoliths in Abyssinia, erected by the race when it passed from Arabia to Africa, have carved in their faces little doors, for the ingress and egress of the spirits. Holed menhirs are found in many places. I know one in France, La Pierre Fiche, near Pouancé (Maine-et-Loire), where such a little door or window, intended for the popping out and in of the spirit, has been utilised to hold an image of the Virgin, and has been barred to prevent the statue making off or being made off with.

In Irish post-Christian records there is frequent allusion to the early saints carrying about their *lechs* (flat stones) with them, to be set up over them when dead, and this explains the fantastic stories afterwards told of saints as of having crossed from Ireland to Wales, or Cornwall, or Brittany floating on stones. In the original record it was related that the saint came over with his *lech*, and a later redactor of the story converted this into coming *on* it, as a raft. The *lech* was cut into a cross when the Celts became Christians, or crosses were inscribed on them. Some of the most fantastic of the saints, when travelling over the country, would not sit down to dinner till they had visited and prayed at all the crosses set up over tombs anywhere near.

A pretty story is told of S. Cainnech. Bishop Aed's sister had been carried off by Colman MacDermot, King of the Hy Niall, and he refused to surrender her. Aed went to Cainnech with his grievance, and Cainnech at once resolved on intervention. Colman had retired to an island in the Ross Lake, or Marsh, and shrewdly suspecting that the saint would administer a lecture, he removed the boats to the island fort or crannoge. However, Cainnech was not to be deterred, and managed to wade or swim across. Subdued by his pertinacity, the king surrendered the girl.

Many years after, one winter day, Cainnech was traversing a moor, when he noticed a rude stone cross, on the head and arms of which the snow lay

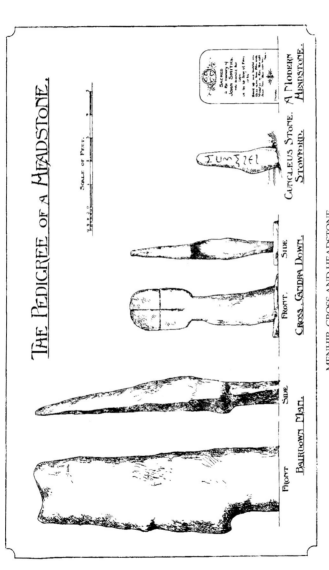

THE PEDIGREE OF A HEADSTONE.

SCALE OF FEET:

FRONT. SIDE.
BARROWN MAEN.

FRONT. SIDE.
CROSS. GULVAL DOWN.

CUTGLEUS STONE.
STOWFORD.

SACRED
to the memory of
JOHN SMITH,

A MODERN
HEADSTONE.

MENHIR, CROSS AND HEADSTONE

in a crust. He halted to inquire whose cross that was, and learned that it had been erected on the spot where King Colman had been assassinated some years previously. Cainnech at once went to the *lech*, leaned his brow against it, and as he recalled the

CROSS, WHITCHURCH DOWN.

interviews he had had with the king, and thought on his good as well as his bad qualities, his outbursts of violence, and his accesses of compunction, the old man's tears began to flow, and his disciples noticed the snow melting and dripping from the arms of the cross, thawed by the tears of the venerable abbot.

Now see how many rugged crosses there are on

Dartmoor! Some certainly are waymarks, others
as surely indicate graves. Would that we knew the
tales connected with them!

Then go into any churchyard and observe the
tombstones. We are children of the men who set
up menhirs, and we do the same thing to this day,
though the stones we erect are mean and small compared with the great standing monoliths they set up
to their dead.

In many of the churches around the moor are
monuments that derive from the cromlech and kistvaens as certainly as does the modern tombstone
from the menhir. The graveyard of Sourton was
rich in these great slabs standing on four supporters.
A late rector who "restored" Sourton church, and
supposed he did God service by so doing, threw all
these down and employed the slabs as pavement to
the church paths; he placed the supporters outside
in the village for anyone to carry off as he listed.

The finest menhirs on Dartmoor are — one at
Drizzlecombe, the Langstone near Caistor Rock,
the Whitmoor Stone, the Bairdown Man, the Langstone at Merrivale, and that on Langstone Moor
Peter Tavy. There must have been numbers more,
for their former presence is testified to by many
place names. They have been carried off, and it
is matter of wonder that any remain.

6. *Hut circles.* The cairn and kistvaen were
the places of burial of the dead, but the hut circles
were the habitations of the living. So many of them
have been dug out during the last six years, that we
may safely draw conclusions as to the period to

which they belong. They were occupied by the
Neolithic population that at one time thickly covered
Dartmoor.

In the *Archæologia* of 1875 is an account of the

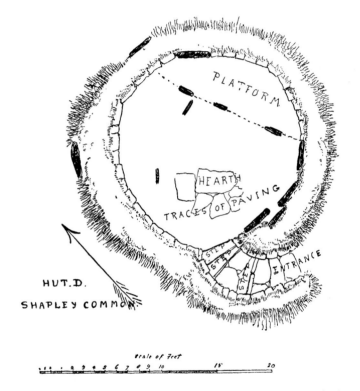

HUT.D.

SHAPLEY COMMON.

Scale of Feet

exploration of a set of hut circles near Bintley,
Northumberland, and this revealed successive occu-
pation by Celts (?) of the Bronze Age; then Romano-
British, who left fragments of Samian ware and a

bronze horse - buckle; lastly by Saxons, who left behind an iron sword.

Not a trace of continuous occupation has been found in any circle explored on Dartmoor. All belong to the early Bronze Period, when flint was the principal material of which tools and weapons were fabricated.

Some account of these huts has been already given. They usually have a raised platform on the side that is towards the hill, and the circle bulges at this point to give additional space on this platform. It was probably used as a bed by night, and was sat upon by day. In one hut at Grimspound the platform was divided into two compartments. In some instances, small upright stones planted in the floor show that the platform was made of logs and brushwood, held in place by these projections. The stone platforms on the other hand were paved.

The doorways into the huts are composed of single upright stones as jambs, with a threshold and a lintel, this latter always fallen, and often found wedged between the uprights. The floor within is paved near the door, but there only; the rest consists of hard beaten soil. Occasionally a shelter wall protects the entrance from the prevailing wind. The huts must have been entered on all-fours; the doorways are never higher than three feet six inches, usually less. The huts have hearthstones much burnt or broken, but occasionally hollows lined with stones full of ashes. Cooking-holes are sunk in the floor near the hearths, and piles of cooking stones are found at hand much cracked by fire. Sometimes

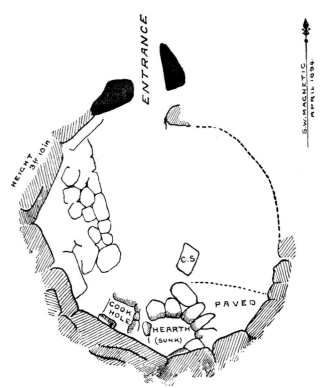

CIRCLE Nº VII

labels within figure: ENTRANCE · HEIGHT 3ft 10in · C.S · COOK HOLE · HEARTH (SUNK) · PAVED · S.W. MAGNETIC APRIL 1894.

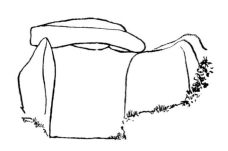

ELEVATION OF ENTRANCE

HUT CIRCLE, GRIMSPOUND.

a flat stone is found bedded in the soil near the centre
to support a pole that sustained the roof. In some
instances a hole has been discovered sunk in the
floor near the middle, with the charred remains of
the bottom end of the post in it.

In the cooking-holes have been found cooking-pots
made by hand of the coarsest clay, usually round at
the bottom ; where not round, with transverse ridges
of thick clay forming a cross to strengthen the
bottom. These pots were too fragile to stand the
action of fire on a hearth, and served by having
meat and red-hot stones placed in them. Consequently they do not show signs of exposure to
strong fire externally, and are black with animal
matter within, which may be extracted by means
of a blowpipe.

One found at Legis Tor had been cracked and
was mended with china-clay. It had a cooking-stone
in it. There would seem to have been in use as well
shallower vessels that were covered with round slate
discs. None of these have been recovered whole.
Possibly they were employed to hold curd or butter.

Occasionally round stones, flat on one side and
convex on the other, have been disinterred in the
huts. They served to protect the apex of the roof,
where the poles were drawn together, from the action
of the rain, which would rot them, as well as to
prevent the rain from entering at this point. An
example of a stone of the same character employed
for this very purpose may be seen in actual use
on a thatched circular pounding-house on Berry
Down, near Throwleigh.

Not a single quern has been found in a hut, and this indicates that the occupants neither grew nor ground corn extensively.* They lived mainly on milk and meat. Numerous rubber-stones have been unearthed that served for smoothing the seams of skin clothing sewn together; and plenty of flint scrapers that turn up show that the skins employed for garments were previously carefully scraped and cleaned. Esquimaux women chew the leather to get it flexible, and then rub it with similar smoothers of stone.

7. *Tracklines* in abundance are everywhere found, made of stones, but without close investigation it is not possible to determine to what period they belong.

8. Paved roads exist; the main road across the moor has been traced from Wray Barton in Moreton Hampstead, by Berry Pound to Merripit, by Post Bridge, and thence on to Mis Tor. From somewhere near the Powder Mills a branch struck off in the direction of Princetown, aiming probably for Tamerton, but it has been obliterated by the prison inclosures. A raised paved road leaves the camp above Okehampton Station and takes a direction due south, but cannot be traced far. That these ways were not Roman is tolerably certain. The ancient Britons drove chariots with wheels, and where wheeled conveyances were in use, there roads are postulated.

9. The *cairns* that are abundant, and were of considerable size, have nearly all been ransacked by treasure-seekers. Only such as were too small to

* Querns have been found, but none in prehistoric habitations.

attract attention have escaped.   They are mounds of earth and stone over a pit sunk in the original soil, or over a kistvaen.   Usually they contain a handful of ashes only; they rarely yield more.   One, however, on Hamildon surrendered a bronze knife with amber handle and rivets of gold.   Others have given up small knives of bronze, and urns of the character-istic shape and ornamentation of the Bronze Age. In one, on Fernworthy Common, was found a thin blade of copper, along with a flint knife, a large button of horn, and a well-ornamented urn.

A cairn surrounded by a circle of stones, and containing a kistvaen, near Princetown, is called "The Crock of Gold," a name that may be due to a vessel of the precious metal having been found in it.

One thing is obvious, the enormous labour of exploring the larger cairns would not have been undertaken unless previous ransackings had yielded valuable results.   Some of the cairns must have been huge, and have taken many men several days in clearing out their interiors.   About these cairns I shall say a good deal in a chapter apart.

10. Of *camps* there are two kinds, those constructed of stone and those of earth   I reserve what I have to say about these to a separate chapter.

11. The old stone *bridges,* composed of rude slabs cast across an opening to a pier, also rudely con-structed, have been attributed to "the Druids," of course.   There is nothing to indicate for these a great antiquity.   They belong to the period of pack-horses, and were doubtless often repaired.   Those

at Dartmeet, and Post Bridge, and Two Bridges
—this last has disappeared—were in the line of
the pack-horse track, and *not* in that of the paved
way across the moor.

The rude bridge at Okery in like manner is in the
pack-horse line of way, which is indicated between
Princetown and Merrivale Bridge by rude posts of
granite set up at intervals.

CHAPTER V.

THE FREAKS

Lucubrations of antiquaries in past times—How their imagination led them astray—Rock idols—Logan stones—Who originated the idea that they were oracular—Rock basins—Tolmens—The difference between the modern system of archæological research and that which it has supplanted.

IT would be amusing were it not melancholy to read the lucubrations of antiquaries of the early part of the nineteenth century on the relics of the past found in such abundance on the moor. Their imagination played a large part in their researches, and references to curious customs in the Bible or in classic writings were drawn in to explain these relics. The antiquaries lacked the faculty of observing accurately, and instead of labouring to accumulate facts, and recording them with precision, employed them as pegs on which to hang their theories, and they whittled at what they did observe, so as to fit what they saw to elucidate these theories.

In rambling over the moor they discovered rock idols, logan stones, rock basins, and tolmens, and entered into long dissertations on their employment for worship, oracles, lustrations, and ordeals.

There are, indeed, to be seen curious piles of rock, but none of these are artificial, and there is not a

BOWERMAN'S NOSE

particle of evidence that any of them received idolatrous worship. Bowerman's Nose is the most remarkable, perhaps. Carrington, the poet of Dartmoor, thus describes it :—

> " On the very edge
> Of the vast moorland, startling every eye,
> A shape enormous rises ! High it towers
> Above the hill's bold brow, and seen from far,
> Assumes the human form ; a granite god,—
> To whom, in days long flown, the suppliant knee
> In trembling homage bow'd."

It stands up, a core of hard granite, forty feet high, in five layers above a " clitter," the softer masses that have fallen off from it. Had it ever been venerated as an idol, the worshippers would assuredly have done something towards clearing this clitter away, so as to give themselves a means of easy access to their idol, and some turf on which to kneel in adoration.

Another remarkable pile is Vixen Tor, presenting from one point a resemblance to the Sphinx. Not a single relic of early man is in its immediate neighbourhood. We can hardly doubt that prehistoric man was not as big a fool as we suppose him, and that he was quite able to see that Bowerman's Nose and Vixen Tor were natural objects as truly as the tors on the hilltops.

The logan stones on the moor are numerous, and these, also, are natural formations. The granite weathers irregularly ; a hard bed alternates with one that is soft, and the wind and rain eat into the more crumbling layer and gnaw it away, till the harder superincumbent mass rests on one or two points. Either it topples over and becomes one more block in a clitter, or it remains balanced, and, if fairly evenly balanced, can be made to rock like a cradle.

Here is a specimen of tall twaddle from the hand of Mrs. Bray or the Rev. E. Atkyns Bray, her husband :—

"There must have been a.more than ordinary feeling of awe inspired in the mind of the criminal by ascending heights covered with a multitude, to whose gaze he was exposed, as he drew nigh and looked upon these massive rocks, the seat of divine authority and judgment. How imposing must have been the sight of the priesthood and their numerous trains, surrounded by all the outward pomps and insignia of their office ; as he listened to the solemn hymns of the vates, preparatory to the ceremonial of justice ; or as he stepped within the sacred inclosure, there to receive condemnation or acquittal, to be referred to the ordeal of the logan, or the tolmen, according to the will of the presiding priest ! As he slowly advanced and thought upon these things, often must he have shuddered and trembled to meet the Druid's eye, when he stood by 'the stone of his power.'"

All this rubbish is based on supposition. There is not a particle of evidence to support it. Toland was the first to start the theory that logan stones were used for ordeal purposes or as oracles. He says: "The Druids made the people believe that they alone could move these stones, and by a miracle only, by which pretended power they condemned or acquitted the accused, and often brought criminals to confess what could in no other way be extorted from them." Here is a positive statement. Toland died in 1722. Whence did Toland derive this? From his imagination only. Then Rowe quotes him as his authority for attributing to the logan stones this function of delivering oracular judgments. Appeal was wont to be made to a line in Ossian as a support

LOGAN ROCK. THE RUGGLESTONE, WIDDECOMBE.

for the theory, but since Ossian has been proved to be a fraud antiquaries are chary of referring to him.

There are some really fine logan rocks on Dartmoor. Perhaps the largest is one above the West Okement, which I remember seeing many years ago, when a boy, rolling in a strong wind like a boat at sea. That on Rippon Tor measures 16½ feet in length, and is about 4½ feet in thickness and nearly the same in breadth. It still logs, but not so well as formerly, owing to mischievous interference with it.

There is a large one in the Teign, above Fingle
Bridge, that can also be made to roll with the
application of a little strength.

The Rugglestone, near Widdecombe-in-the-Moor,
measures 22 feet by 14 feet in one part, and 19 feet
by 17 feet in another, and is 5 feet 6 inches in mean
thickness. Its computed weight is 110 tons, whereas
the celebrated logan in Cornwall weighs 90 tons.
This stone is poised upon two points.

Roos Tor, which the Ordnance surveyors playfully
render Rolls Tor, possessed two logan stones, but
quarrymen have destroyed one, together with the
fine mass of rock on which it stood. Near it
lay a huge menhir, never removed till these depre-
dators broke it up. I give an illustration of the
head of the tor with its two logans, taken in 1852;
one alone remains. On Black Tor, near the road
from Princetown to Plymouth, is a small logan, with
a rock basin on the top, and with a projection like
a handle. It can be made to oscillate without
difficulty. A small logan is near the stone rows on
Challacombe in the miners' workings. Its existence
is purely accidental. Another is near a collection
of hut circles on the slope of Combeshead Tor.

The rock basins are numerous; they are hollow
pans formed on the surface of granite slabs by the
action of wind and water, assisted by particles of
grit set in rotation by the wind. " That this rude
and primitive species of basin formed part of the
apparatus of Druidism there can be little doubt,"
says Mr. Rowe, " but the specific purpose for which
they were designed is not clear." Fosbroke un-

hesitatingly pronounces rock basins to be "cavities *cut* in the surface of a rock, supposed for reservoirs, to preserve the rain or dew in its original purity, for the religious uses of the Druids."

All this assertion must be put aside. The bowls are excavated by natural agencies, and there is not a scrap of evidence to show that they were put to superstitious or any other use. The largest is on Caistor Rock, and this has been railed round, as

ROOS TOR, WITH ITS LOGANS, PREVIOUS TO DESTRUCTION.

sheep floundered in and got drowned, or could not get out again. Mis Tor has a fine basin, called " The Devil's Frying-pan."

These basins may be seen in all stages of growth on the tops of the tors.

The tolmen is either a holed stone or a rock supported in such a manner as to preserve it from falling, and supposed to have been used as an apparatus of ordeal, by requiring those accused of a crime to creep through the orifice.

Holed stones have unquestionably been employed for the purpose of taking oaths and sealing compacts, the hands being passed through an opening and clasped. And certainly S. Wilfrid's needle, in the crypt under Ripon Minster, was made use of as a test to try whether a maiden accused of incontinency was guilty or not. There is, however, no well-defined tolmen on Dartmoor that can be pronounced to be artificial. A holed stone in the Teign was pierced by the action of the water, and a suspended rock at an incline on Staple Tor, called by Mrs. Bray and Mr. Rowe a tolmen, is a natural production also. It is, of course, possible that stones thus poised may have been employed for the purpose, but we have no evidence that those on Dartmoor were so used.

Of rocks supported at one end by a small stone there are plenty. There is a good one on Yar Tor, above Dartmeet.

The old school of antiquaries started with a theory, and then sought for illustrations to fit into their theories, and took facts and distorted them to serve their purpose, or saw proofs where no proofs existed. The new school accumulates statistics and piles up facts, and then only endeavours to work out a plausible theory to account for the facts laboriously collected and registered. It never starts with a theory, but applies practices in savage life still in use to explain the customs of prehistoric men, who lived on the same cultural level as the savages of the present day.

One word of caution must be given relative to the Druids, who are credited with so much. It is true that there were Druids in Britain and in Ireland, but they were the schamans, or medicine-men, of the earlier Ivernian race, who maintained their repute among the conquering Celts, and their representatives at the present day are the white witches who practise on the credulity of our villagers.

CHAPTER VI.

DEAD MEN'S DUST

Cairns on Dartmoor—Why mostly in solitary places and on hilltops—
The theory of wearing mourning—Its real origin—Various modes
of deceiving the dead or discouraging them from returning—The
desire of the ghost to get home—Is cajoled or scared away—How
widows get rid of the ghosts of their first husbands—Disguising
the dead.

ONE of the most striking experiences of an
explorer of Dartmoor is the coming upon
great cairns in the most remote and inaccessible
parts of that waste. Not a lone hill surrounded by
bogs is without its great mound of earth or pile of
stones over some dead man. In the howling wilderness about Cranmere Pool, where are no traces of
human habitation, there lie the dead. On every rise
above the swamps and fathomless morasses of Fox
Tor, there they are scattered thick. Almost always
the dead were conveyed to the tops of hills, or
placed on the brows of elevations far away from the
settlements of the living.

Why was this?

Because prehistoric men were in fear of their dead
people.

I remember, in 1860, riding across the central
desert of Iceland, and coming about midnight, when

the summer sun was just dipped below the polar sea, on a solitary cairn among pools of frozen water and amidst illimitable tracts of volcanic ash. My guide told me it was the grave of one Glamr, who had so haunted the farms in the Vatnsdal that the people of the valley had combined to dig him up and transport the corpse almost a day's journey into the central desert, where they cut off his head, and buried the body in a sitting posture with his own skull as his throne, an indignity which the ghost was likely to so resent as never to venture to show again.

The heathen Icelander, on the death of a father in the family, was removed by the anxious heir to the estate in an ingenious manner. The wall of the house behind the bed was broken through, and the corpse drawn out of doors by that way, and then the opening was hastily repaired. He was then hurried off to his grave. The heir was so afraid lest the venerable party should saunter home again and re-claim his property, that the father was carried forth in this peculiar manner in order to bewilder him and make him find a difficulty in returning.

A strip of black cloth an inch and a half in width stitched round the sleeve—that is the final, or per-haps penultimate relic (for it may dwindle further to a black thread) of the usage of wearing mourning on the decease of a relative.

The usage is one that commends itself to us as an outward and visible sign of the inward sentiment of bereavement, and not one in ten thousand who adopt mourning has any idea that it ever possessed a signification of another sort. And yet the correla-

tion of general custom—of mourning fashions—
leads us to the inexorable conclusion that in its in-
ception the practice had quite a different signification
from that now attributed to it, nay more, that it is
solely because its primitive meaning has been absolutely forgotten, and an entirely novel significance
given to it, that mourning is still employed after a
death.

Look back through the telescope of anthropology
at our ancestors in their naked savagery after a death,
and we see them daub themselves with soot mingled
with tallow. When the savage assumed clothes and
became a civilised man, he replaced the fat and lampblack with black cloth, and this black cloth has
descended to us in the nineteenth century as the
customary and intelligible trappings of woe.

The Chinaman when in a condition of bereavement assumes white garments, and we may be pretty
certain that his barbarous ancestor, like the Anda-
man Islander of the present day, pipe-clayed his
naked body after the decease and funeral of a
relative. In Egypt yellow was the symbol of sorrow
for a death, and that points back to the ancestral nude
Egyptian having smeared himself with yellow ochre.

Black was not the universal hue of mourning in
Europe. In Castile white obtained on the death of
its princes. Herrera states that the last time white
was thus employed was in 1498 on the death of
Prince John. This use of white indicates chalk or
pipe-clay as the daub affected by the ancestors of
the house of Castile in primeval time as a badge
of bereavement.

Various explanations have been offered to account for the variance of colour. White has been supposed to denote purity—and to this day white gloves and hatbands and scarves are employed at the funeral of a young girl.

Yellow has been supposed to symbolise that death is the end of human hopes, because falling leaves are sere ; black is taken as the privation of light ; and purple or violet also affected as a blending of joy with sorrow. Christian moralists have declaimed against black as heathen, as denoting an aspect of death devoid of hope, and gradually purple is taking its place in the trappings of the hearse, if not of the mourners, and the pall is now very generally violet.

But these explanations are after-thoughts, and an attempt to give reason for the divergence of usage which might satisfy : they are really no explanations at all. The usage goes back to a period when there were no such refinements of thought. If violet or purple has been traditional, it is so merely because the ancestral Briton stained himself with woad on the death of a relative.

The pipe-clay, lampblack, yellow ochre, and woad of the primeval mourners must be brought into range with a whole series of other mourning usages, and then the result is something of an " eye-opener." It reveals a condition of mind and an aspect of death that cause not a little surprise and amusement. It is one of the most astonishing, and, perhaps, shocking traits of barbarous life, that death revolutionises completely the feelings of the survivors towards their deceased husbands, wives, parents, and other relatives.

A married couple may have been sincerely attached to each other so long as the vital spark was twinkling, but the moment it is extinguished the dead partner becomes, not a sadly sweet reminiscence, but an object of the liveliest terror to the survivor. He or she does everything that ingenuity can suggest to get himself or herself out of all association in body and spirit with the late lamented. Death is held to be thoroughly demoralising to the deceased. However exemplary a person he or she may have been in life, after death the ghost is little less than a plaguing, spiteful spirit.

There is in the savage no tender clinging to the remembrance of the loved one; he is transformed into a terrible bugbear, who must be evaded and avoided by every contrivance conceivable. This is due, doubtless, mainly to the inability of the uncultivated mind to discriminate between what is seen waking from what presents itself in phantasy to the dreaming head. After a funeral it is natural enough for the mourners to dream of the dead, and they at once conclude that they have been visited by his *revenant*. After a funeral feast—a great gorging of pork or beef—it is very natural that the sense of oppression and pain felt should be associated with the dear departed, and should translate itself into the idea that he has come from his grave to sit on the chests of those who have bewailed him.

Moreover, the savage associates the idea of desolation, death, discomfort, with the condition of the soul after death, and believes that the ghosts do all they can to return to their former haunts and associates for the sake of the warmth and food, the shelter of the huts, and the entertainment of the society of their fellows. But the living men and women are not at all eager to receive the ghosts into the family circle, and they accordingly adopt all kinds of "dodges," expedients to prevent the departed from making these irksome and undesired visits.

The Venerable Bede tells us that Laurence, Archbishop of Canterbury, resolved on flying from England because he was hopeless of effecting any good under the successor of Ethelbert, King of Kent. The night before he fled he slept on the floor of the church, and dreamed that S. Peter cudgelled him soundly for resolving to abandon his sacred charge. In the morning he awoke stiff and full of aches and pains. Turned into modern language we should say that Archbishop Laurence was attacked with rheumatism on account of his having slept on the cold stones of the church. His mind had been troubled before he went to sleep with doubts whether he was doing right in abandoning his duty, and very naturally this trouble of conscience coloured his dream and gave to his rheumatic twinges the complexion they assumed in his mind.

Now Archbishop Laurence regarded the Prince of the Apostles in precisely the light in which a savage views his deceased relatives and ancestors. He associates his maladies, his pains, with them, if he should happen to dream of them. If, however, when in pain, he dreams of a living person, then he holds that this living person has cast a magical spell over him.

Among Nature's men, before they have gone through the mill of civilisation, plenty to eat and to drink, and someone to talk to, are the essentials of happiness. They see that the dead have none of these requisites, they consider that they are miserable without them. The writer remembers how, when he was a boy, and attended the funeral of a relative in November, he could not sleep all night—a bitter frosty night—with the thought how cold it must be to the dead in the vault, without blankets, hot bottle, or fire. It was in vain for him to reason against the feeling; the feeling was so strong in him that he was conscious of an uncomfortable expectation of the dead coming to claim a share of the blanket, fire, or hot bottle. Now the savage never reasons against such a feeling, and he assumes that the dead will return, as a matter of course, for what he cannot have in the grave.

The ghost is very anxious to assert its former rights. A widow has to get rid of the ghost of her first husband before she can marry again. In Parma a widow about to be remarried is pelted with sticks and stones, not in the least because the Parmese object to remarriage, but in order to scare away the ghost of number one who is hanging about his wife, and who will resent his displacement in her affections by number two.

To the present day, in some of the villages of the ancient Duchy of Teck, in Würtemberg, it is customary when a corpse is being conveyed to the cemetery for the relatives and friends to surround the dead, and in turn talk to it—assure it what a blessed rest it

is going to; how anxious the kinsfolk are that it
may be comfortable; how handsome will be the cross
set over the grave; how much all desire that it may
sleep soundly and not by any means leave the grave
and come haunting old scenes and friends; how un-
reasonable such conduct as the latter hinted at would
be—how it would alter the regard entertained for the
deceased, how disrespectful to the Almighty who
gives rest to the good, and how it would be regarded
as an admission of an uneasy conscience.   Lively
comparisons are drawn between the joys of paradise
and the vale of tears that has been quitted, so as to
take away from the deceased all desire to return.

This is a survival of primitive usage and mode
of thought, and has its analogies in many places and
among diverse races.

The Dacotah Indians address the ghost of the
dead in the same "soft solder" to induce it to take
the road to the world of spirits, and not to come
sauntering back to its wigwam.   In Siam and in
China it is much the same; persuasion, flattery,
threats, are employed.

Unhappily, all ghosts are not open to persuasion,
and see through the designs of the mourners, and
with them severer measures have to be resorted to.
Among the Slavs of the Danube and the Czechs,
the bereaved, after the funeral, on going home, turn
themselves about after every few steps, and throw
sticks, stones, mud, even hot coals, in the direction
of the churchyard, so as to frighten the spirit back
to the grave so considerately provided for it.   A
Finnish tribe has not even the decency to wait till

the corpse is covered with soil ; they fire pistols and guns after it as it goes to its grave.

In *Hamlet,* at the funeral of Ophelia, the priest says :—

> " For charitable prayers,
> Shards, flints, and pebbles should be thrown on her."

Unquestionably it must have been customary in England thus to pelt a ghost that was suspected of the intention to wander. The stake driven through the suicide's body was a summary way of ensuring that his ghost should not be troublesome.

Those Finns who fired guns after a dead man had another expedient for holding him fast, if the first failed, and that was to nail him down in his coffin. The Arabs tie his legs together. The Wallachs drive a long nail through his skull ; and this usage explains the many skulls that have been exhumed in Germany thus perforated.

The Californian Indians were wont to break the spine of the corpse so as to paralyse his lower limbs and make "walking" impossible. Spirit and body, to the unreasoning mind, are intimately associated. A hurt done to the body wounds the soul. Mrs. Crowe, in her *Night Side of Nature*, tells a story reversing this. A gentleman in Germany was dying. He expressed great desire to see his son, who was a ne'er-do-well, and was squandering his money in Paris. At that time the young man was sitting on a bench in the Bois-de-Boulogne, with a switch in his hand. Suddenly, he beheld his old father before him. Convinced that he saw a phantom, he raised his switch, and cut the apparition once, twice, and thrice across the face, and it vanished. At that moment the dying father uttered a scream, and held his hands to his face. "My boy! my boy! He is striking me again — again!" and he died. The Algonquin Indians beat the walls of the death-chamber to drive out the ghost. In Sumatra a priest is employed with a broom to sweep the ghost out. In Scotland and in North Germany the chairs on which a coffin has rested are reversed, lest the dead man should take a fancy to sit on them instead of going to his grave. In ancient Mexico certain pro-fessional ghost ejectors were employed, who, after a funeral, were invited to visit and thoroughly ex-plore the house whence the dead had been removed, and if they found the ghost lurking about in corners, in cupboards, under beds—anywhere, to kick it out. In Siberia, after forty days' "law" given to the ghost, if it be still found loafing about, the Schaman is sent for, who drums it out. He extorts brandy, which he professes to require, as he has to personally conduct the deceased to the land of spirits, where he will make it and the other ghosts so fuddled that they will forget the way back to earth.

In North Germany a troublesome ghost is bagged, and the bag is emptied in some lone spot, or in the garden of a neighbour against whom a grudge is entertained.

Another mode of getting rid of the spirit of the dear departed is to confuse it as to its way home. This is done in various ways. Sometimes the road by which it has been carried to its resting-place is swept to efface the footprints, and a false track is made into a wood or on to a moor so that the ghost may take the wrong road. Sometimes ashes are strewn on the way to hide the footprints. Sometimes the dead is carried rapidly three or four times round the house so as to make him giddy and not know in which direction he is carried.* The universal practice of closing the eyes of the dead may be taken to have originated in the desire that he might be prevented from seeing his way.

In places it was, as already said, customary for the dead body to be taken out of the house, not through the door, but by a hole knocked in the wall for the purpose, and backwards. In Corea, blinders made of black silk are put on the dead man's eyes, to prevent him from finding his way home.

Many savage nations entirely abandon a hut or a camp in which a death has occurred for precisely the same reason—of throwing the dead man's spirit into confusion as to its way home.

It was a common practice in England till quite recently for the room in which a death had occurred to be closed for some time, and this is merely a survival of the custom of abandoning the place where a spirit has left the body. The Esquimaux take out their dying relatives to huts constructed of blocks of ice or snow, and leave them there to expire, for ghosts are as stupid as they are trouble-

---

* This was done at Manaton at every funeral, the only difference being that he was carried round and round the cross. A former rector, Rev. C. Carwithen, destroyed the cross so as to put a stop to this practice.

some ; they have no more wits than a peacock, they can only find their way to the place where they died.

Other usages are to divert a stream and bury the corpse in the river-bed, or lay it beyond running water, which, according to ghost-lore, it cannot pass. Or, again, fires are lighted across its path, and it shrinks from passing through flames. As for water, ghosts loathe it. Among the Matamba negroes a widow is flung into the water and dipped repeatedly so as to wash off the ghost of the dead husband, which is supposed to be clinging to her. In New Zealand, among the Maoris, all who have followed the corpse dive into water so as to throw off the ghost which is sneaking home after them. In Tahiti, all who have assisted at a burial run as hard as they can to the sea and take headers into it for the same object. It is the same in New Guinea. We see the same idea reduced to a mere form in ancient Rome, where, in place of the dive through water, a vessel of water was carried twice round those who had followed the corpse, and they were sprinkled. The custom of washing for purification after a funeral practised by the Jews is a reminiscence of the usage, with a novel explanation given to it.

In the South Pacific, in the Hervey Islands, after a death, men turn out to pummel and fight the returning spirit, and give it a good drubbing in the air.

Now perhaps the reader may have been brought to understand what the sundry mourning costumes originally meant. They were disguises whereby to deceive the ghosts, so that they might not recognise and pester with their undesired attentions the relatives who live. Indians who are wont to paint themselves habitually, go after a funeral totally unbedecked with colour. On the other hand, other savages daub themselves fantastically with various colours, making themselves as unlike to what they were previously as is possible. The Coreans, when in mourning, assume hats with low rims that conceal their features.

The Papuans conceal themselves under extinguishers made of banana leaves. Elsewhere in New Guinea they envelop themselves in a wicker-work frame in which they can hardly walk. Among the Mpongues of Western Africa, those who on ordinary occasions wear garments, when suffering bereavement walk in complete nudity. Valerius Maximus tells us that among the Lycians it was customary in mourning for the men to disguise themselves in women's garments.

The custom of cutting the hair short, and of scratching and disfiguring the face, and of rending the garments, all originated from the same thought —to make the survivors unrecognisable by the ghost of the deceased. Plutarch asserts that the Sacæ, after a death, went down into pits and hid themselves for days from the light of the sun. Australian widows near the north-west bend of the Murray shave their heads and plaster them with pipe-clay, which, when dry, forms a close-fitting skull-cap. The spirit of the late lamented, on returning to his better half, either does not recognise his spouse, or is so disgusted with her appearance that he leaves her for ever.

There is almost no end to the expedients adopted

for getting rid of the dead. Piles of stones are heaped over them, they are buried deep in the earth, they are walled up in natural caves, they are inclosed in megalithic structures, they are burned, they are sunk in the sea. They are threatened, they are cajoled, they are hoodwinked. Every sort of trickery is had recourse to to throw them off the scent of home and to displease them with their living relations.

The wives, horses, dogs slain and buried with them, the copious supplies of food and drink laid on their graves, are bribes to induce them to be content with their situation. Nay, further, in very many places no food may be eaten in the house of mourning for many days after an interment. The object, of course, is to disappoint the returning spirit, which comes seeking a meal, finds none; comes again next day, finds none again ; and after a while out of sheer disgust desists from returning.

A vast amount of misdirected ingenuity is expended in bamboozling and bullying the unhappy ghosts ; but the feature most striking in these proceedings is the unanimous agreement in considering these ghosts as such imbeciles. When they put off their outward husk, they divest themselves of all that cunning which is the form that intelligence takes in the savage. Not only so, but, although they remember and crave after home comforts, they absolutely forget the tricks they had themselves played on the souls of the dead in their own lifetime ; they walk and blunder into the traps which they had themselves laid for other ghosts in the days of their flesh.

Perhaps the lowest abyss of dunderheadedness they have been supposed to reach is when made to mistake their own identity. Recently, near Mentone, a series of prehistoric interments in caves has been exposed. They reveal the dead men as having had their heads daubed over with red oxide of iron. Still extant races of savages paint, plaster, and disfigure their dead. The prehistoric Greeks masked them. The Aztecs masked their deceased kings, and the Siamese do so still. We cannot say with absolute certainty what the object is, but we are probably not far out when we conjecture the purpose to be to make the dead forget who they are when they look at their reflection in the water. There was a favourite song sung some sixty years ago relative to a little old woman who got "muzzy." Whilst in this condition some naughty boys cut her skirts at her knees. When she woke up and saw her condition, "Lawk!" said the little old woman, "this never is me!" And certain ancient peoples treated their dead in something the same way; they disguised and disfigured them so that each ghost on waking up might exclaim, "Lawk! this never is me!" And so, having lost its identity, the soul did not consider that it had a right to revisit its old home and molest its old acquaintances.

PLAN OF WHITTOR CAMP

CHAPTER VII.

THE CAMPS

No camps in the forest—All on the confines—No apprehension of
attack from the south—Whit Tor—The exploration of the camp
—How the walls were constructed—This explains their ruinous
condition—Brent Tor formerly a camp—How a road up it was made
—The Dewerstone camp—Earthen camps—Hembury—The Galford
Down camp—A Saxon thegn's burrh—Old Squire Bidlake—Lydford fortifications.

A S I have already said, the inhabitants of Dartmoor in prehistoric times seem to have been
of a peaceable disposition. There are pounds to
contain cattle and protect them against wolves, but
no camps on the moor itself. What camps there
are will be found on its confines, as though the
natives feared attack from an enemy outside, but
were not troubled by their neighbours of the same
blood and pursuits.

Of camps there are two sorts, but we cannot be
sure that they belong to different races of men.
The stone-walled fortresses are few—Brent Tor, Whit
Tor, Cranbrook, one near Ashburton, and the Dewerstone. Of earth, or earth and stone mixed, there
are more. A small one above Tavistock, an immense
and very important one at Galford or Burleigh in
Bridestowe, one above the station at Okehampton,

97

Wooston and Prestonbury on the Teign, Holne and Hembury on the Dart. Along the south of the moor are none till we reach Boringdon, between the Plym and the Tory. But one only of all these has been systematically explored, and that is, perhaps, the finest, on Whit Tor, above Mary and Peter Tavy.

Whit Tor rises to the height of 1,526 feet above the sea-level. It is on Cudlipptown Down, and commands exceedingly fine views westward as far as the distant Cornish hills.

The tor is not of granite, but of gabbro, an eruptive igneous rock, very black and hard, and splitting along defined planes under the action of the weather. The north side near the summit is covered with a clitter of broken masses.

The boldest masses of rock rise on the south precipitously, but there are fangs of rock that shoot up over the small plateau that forms the summit of the hill.

The whole of the summit is surrounded by a double wall in a very ruinous condition, and this is to a considerable extent due to the smallness of the stones of which it was composed. The faces of the walls were to be traced only by digging, and were never more than doubtful.

Both walls appear to have been 10 feet thick, perhaps a little more; the outer, when perfect, might have had a height of 4 to 4½ feet, whilst the inner, judged by the débris, appears to have been 6 to 7 feet high.

The space between the walls varied, owing to the

inequalities of the ground, but was generally 10 feet wide.

The area inclosed by the innermost wall amounts to close on one and a half acres; the total amount included within the outer wall is about two and a half acres of ground.

The circumference is very much broken up, as is also the inclosed area, by considerable masses of protruding rocks. About these, within the camp, heaps of small stones had been piled up, forming cairns. The largest and most notable of these is at the south-west, and consists of a core of rock about which an immense accumulation of stones has been heaped. All these cairns were thoroughly explored. They covered no interments, and although they disclosed evidences that fires had been lighted against the rocks, and that people had camped there for a while, they showed no tokens of structural erection, as though they were ruinous huts built against the native rock. The huge cairn was removed with great labour, and revealed nothing whatever beneath it but one flint flake.

These cairns, there can be little doubt, were collections of stones for the use of the besieged, to serve as missiles, or for the repair of the walls.

Within the area of the camp are a few hut circles. One near the centre is double, and contained an incredible number of flint chips, a flint scraper, and a core from which flakes had been struck. The whole area is littered with flint chips that are brought up by the moles when making their burrows, and curiously enough not a single arrow-head or flake that can be confidently set down as a weapon has been disinterred. The pottery found is all of the hand-made cooking-vessel type.

To the east is a circle sheltered on one side by a mass of rock, that has a second chamber, a sort of bedroom made under a slab of rock, with the interstices on all sides built up, except only on that by which it was entered from the hut. A good deal

COVERED CHAMBER AND COOKING-HOLE.

of flint was found there. Outside, on the south, was another hut circle, where a piece of clear quartz crystal was found, together with a flint knife that had one edge serrated by use.

Connected with the camp on the north-east is a ruined wall that leads to an inclosure with numerous hut circles. South-west of the camp further down the hill is a pound in good preservation with eight hut circles in it. A reeve or bank to the west of the camp leads down to other collections of habitations of the same description.

Some ten cairns on the slopes have been investigated, but have yielded little beyond the handful of ashes sunk in a pit in the centre that represents the dead. A ruined kistvaen, much mutilated, lies between the camp and the Langstone, a menhir that gives its name to the common, and which is the starting-point of a stone row of very inconsiderable blocks that led to a cairn now demolished, and its

CONSTRUCTION OF STONE AND TIMBER WALL.

place occupied by a pool. From Langstone a track to the south-east leads by the head of the Peter Tavy stream, which rises in a bog, to a fine circle of standing stones, and on the slope below that and above the Walkham river is a large settlement of some thirty or forty habitations. Beyond the Peter Tavy brook, moreover, are numerous clusters of dwellings. To all the population who lived in these huts, Whit Tor had served as a camp of refuge. The place deserves a visit, for we have there collected within a small radius the houses and hamlets occupied by the primeval race, the tombs of their dead, the stone row set up in memory of some chief represented by the Longstone towering above the petty stones below, the circle in which the dead were burned, and finally, the camp to which they flew to defend their beloved moor from invasion.

It may cause some surprise that the walls of the stone castles should be in such complete ruin. But, in all likelihood, they were constructed on the same principle as the Gaulish camps described by Cæsar. They were built of timber frames packed in with stones, and the logs mortised together held the stones in place. When, however, the wood rotted, this mode of construction ensured and precipitated utter rüin. At Murcens, in the department of Lot, is one of these stone camps, and sufficiently well preserved, owing to the size of the limestone slabs employed in the building, to show precisely how the whole was constructed. But the walls of Iosolodunum, that held out so bravely against Cæsar, being built of small stones compacted with timber, are now but heaps of ruin, no better than those of Whit Tor.

Brent Tor was fortified in a manner very similar to Whit Tor; the outer wall remains fairly perfect on the north side, but the inner wall has been much injured. In this instance it is not the summit, but the base of the hill that has been defended. As there is a church on the summit, as also a churchyard with its wall, these have drawn their supplies from the circumvallation. Moreover, it has been broken through to form a way up to the church.

BRENT TOR

A late curate of Tavistock, whose function it was to take the service on Brent Tor, and who found it often desperate work to scramble to the summit in storm and sleet and rain, resolved on forming a roadway to the churchyard gate. But he experienced some difficulty in persuading men to go out from Tavistock to work at this churchway. However, he supplied himself with several bottles of whisky, and when he saw a sturdy labourer standing idle in the market-place he invited him into his lodgings and plied him with hot grog, till the man in a moist and smiling condition assented to the proposition that he should give a day to the Brent Tor path. By this means it was made. The curate was wont to say : " Hannibal cut his way through the Alps with vinegar ; I hewed mine over Brent Tor with prime usquebaugh." Few traces of this way remain, but in making it sad mischief was made with the inner wall of the fortress.

On Brent Tor summit it is sometimes impossible to stand against the wind. I remember how that on one occasion a baptismal party mounted it in driving rain. The father carried the child, and he wore for the occasion a new blue jersey. When the poor babe was presented at the font it was not only streaming with water, but its sopped white garments had become blue with the stain from the father's jersey.

On an occasion of a funeral, when the parson emerged from the church door he was all but prostrated by the north-west blast, and he and the funeral party had to proceed to the grave much like frogs. "Crook'y down, sir!" was the sexton's advice; and the whole company had to press forward bent double, and to finish the service seated in the "lew" of headstones.

According to popular belief the graves, which are cut in the volcanic tufa, fill with water, and the dead dissolve into a sort of soup. But this is not true; the rock is dry and porous. It discharges its drainage by a little spring on the north-east that in process of ages has worked itself from stage to stage lower down the hill.

The Dewerstone Camp consists of two stone walls drawn across the headland. No walls were needed for the sides that were precipitous. Cranbrook Castle is in very good preservation, except on the side towards the Teign, where it has been removed by road-menders, but not within recent years. It richly deserves to be investigated, and the owners have recently granted permission to do so to the Dartmoor Exploration Committee.

We come next to the earthen-banked camps. Of these there is a very fine example at Hembury, near Buckfastleigh. But the finest of all is in Burleigh Wood, in the parish of Bridestowe. Here the side accessible from Galford Down has been cut through, with a trench and a bank thrown up on the camp side, and this is carried right across the neck. The earthen banks were almost certainly crested with palisades. Hard by this early camp, where a bronze palstave has been found, is another of a different character, occupying the extreme point of the hill. This consists of a tump or mound, with

an earthwork round it as a ring.   In this are remains
of iron-smelting.

There can be little doubt as to the period of this
latter. It was the *burrh* of the Anglo-Saxon, and
was in every point similar to the *mottes* of the
Merovingians in France.   On the Bayeux tapestry
three fortified places are represented—Dinan, Dol,
and Rennes—and all are of the same type. A mound
of earth was either thrown up, or a hilltop was
artificially shaped like a tumulus.   On the top of
this the *thegn* erected his fortress of wood.   In the
Bayeux representations the superstructures at Dol
and Rennes are of timber, and that of Dinan is
partly of timber and partly of stone. A flying
bridge of wood led from the gate in the palisading
of the outer ring, supported on posts, and conducted
by an incline to the gate of the citadel. An example
of one of these camps at Bishopston in Gower has
been explored recently.*   The stumps of the pales
were there found embedded in the clay of the bank,
in tolerable preservation.

In the valley below Burleigh Camp, commanding
the ancient road from Exeter by Okehampton to
Launceston, was a third camp, that has been for
the most part obliterated ; it occupied a rising knoll
of limestone, and this latter has been quarried, so
that the camp earthworks have been either destroyed
or buried under the accumulations from the quarry.

The locality is of great interest. The ridge goes
by the name of Galford, and there is reason to think

* *Archæologia Cambrensis*, July, 1899. The camp was excavated
by Colonel W. L. Morgan.

that this was the Gavulford of the Anglo-Saxon Chronicle, where, in 823, the Britons made their last stand against Egbert and the Saxons of Devon.

The place is by nature very strong, and it dominates two roads, that from Exeter to Cornwall, and that which branched off from it on Sourton Down and struck through Sourton to Lydford. The name Gavulford signifies the holdfast on the *fordd* or road.

Burleigh Camp is on the estate of Bidlake, an interesting old manor house, long the residence of a family of the same name, and deserving a visit. Old Squire Bidlake was a zealous Royalist, and the Parliamentary soldiers went to his house to seize him. As they entered the avenue they met an elderly tramp in rags, and said, "You fellow. Have you seen Squire Bidlake?"

"Yes," he replied; "I've just come from the house, and when I was there he was in it."

Then he went his way, and not till too late did they discover that this tramp was Squire Bidlake himself slipping away in disguise.

He fled to Burleigh Wood. There is a little farm below it, in which, at the time, lived a tenant of the name of Veale. Veale and his wife and daughter concealed him in the underwood, and daily conveyed to him food, and supplied him with blankets till the search for him ceased.

At the Restoration, Squire Bidlake made over the farm to the Veales on a nominal rent, to be held by them on this rent so long as a male Veale of their descent remained to hold it.

Both Bidlakes and Veales are now gone, and the

little farmhouse is a ruin. Squire Bidlake is supposed still to haunt the wood, and children are frightened by their mothers with the threat that the old squire will come and fetch them, if naughty.

Lydford was strongly defended. It occupies a fringe of land between ravines, and lines of fortification were drawn across the neck. These may still be traced. The castle stands on a tump artificially shaped. Beyond the church is another small camp, probably British. The castle itself is a structure of stone, replacing the old Saxon *burrh*.

It was probably from the bridges leading up into these citadels, which the Norsemen saw when they harried our coasts, that they conceived the idea that the rainbow was the great bridge leading up into Odin's Valhalla.

"What fools the gods must be," says the inquirer in the Edda, "to build their passage of egress and ingress of such brittle stuff."

TIN-STREAMING

NO one who has eyes in his head, and considers what he sees, if he has been on Dartmoor, can have failed to observe how that every stream-bed has been turned over, and how that every hollow in a hillside is furrowed.

The tin-streamers who thus scarred the face of the moor carried on their works far down below where the rivers debouch from the moor on to the lowlands, but there the evidences of their toil have been effaced by culture.

The tin found in the detritus of streams is the oxide, and is far purer than tin found in the lode. Mining for tin was pursued on Dartmoor during the Middle Ages to a limited extent only, and solely when the stream tin was exhausted.

A very interesting excursion may be made from Douseland Station up the Meavy valley to Nosworthy

BLOWING-HOUSE UNDER BLACK TOR

Bridge, above which several old tin-moulds may be seen lying in the track beside the river, and tin-workings are passed. But perhaps the most interesting portion of the walk is that up the Nillacombe that opens on to the Meavy from the right below Kingset.

Above this the stream has been turned about and

TIN-WORKINGS, NILLACOMBE.

its bed torn up, and rubble heaped in huge piles. Not only so, but the hillslope to the south is marked as with confluent smallpox, the result of the gropings of miners after tin. They followed up every trickle from the side and dug *costeening*, or *shoding*, pits everywhere in search of metal.

The upper waters of the Webburn have in like manner been explored, and some idea of the extent to which the moor was lacerated by the miners may be obtained from the Warren Inn on the road

from Post Bridge to Moreton, looking east, when the
slopes of Headland Warren and Challacombe will be
seen seamed deeply.

The remains of the tinners have not been subjected
to as full an exploration as they merit, but certain
results have nevertheless been reached. One thing
is abundantly clear, that all the tin-streaming was
done subsequently to the time when men occupied
the hut circles. The population living in them
knew nothing of tin.

Diodorus Siculus, who wrote B.C. 8, says that the
dwellers at Belerium, a cape of Britain, mined and
smelted tin. "After beating it up into knucklebone
shapes they carry it to a certain island lying off
Britain, named Ictis, for at ebb tides, the space
between drying up, they carry the tin in waggons
thither . . . and thence the merchants buy it from
the inhabitants and carry it over to Gaul, and lastly,
travelling by land through Gaul about thirty days,
they bring down the loads on horses to the mouth
of the Rhine."

There can exist little doubt that Ictis is the same
as Vectis, the Isle of Wight. It is held that anciently
the island was connected with the mainland. The
Roman station and harbour was at Brading. The
early workers first pounded the ore with stone
crushers, and such have been found. They then
fanned it in the wind, which carried off the fine
light dust, and left the metal on the shovels on
which they tossed the ore and grit into the air.
Beside some of the workings heaps of this dust
have been detected. The washing of the ore came

later. When sufficient had been collected, long troughs were sunk in the "calm," or native clay, and these were filled with charcoal; then the tin ore was laid on this charcoal, and either more of this latter was heaped above, or else peat was piled

MORTAR-STONE, OKEFORD.

up, with layers of ore. Finally the whole was kindled. No bellows were used, but a draught through the channel kept the whole glowing, and the metal ran through the fire into the bottom of the hollow, or ran out at the end, as this rude furnace was constructed on an incline.

In Staffordshire, at Kinver, and in the neighbourhood of Stourbridge, in Worcestershire, I have seen
banks and hedges made up of what are locally called
burrs. These consist of masses of sand and iron
slag, two feet in diameter, round, and concave on one
side, convex on the other. These burrs were formed
in the primitive manufacture of iron, which much
resembled that of tin. Andrew Yarranton, in *England's Improvement by Sea and Land*, 1698, says that
he saw dug up near the walls of Worcester the
hearth of an old Roman iron-furnace.

"It was an open hearth upon which was placed alter-
nately charcoal and ironstone, to which fire being applied ;
it was urged by men treading upon bellows. The operation was very slow and imperfect. Unless the ore was very
rich, not more than one hundredweight of iron could be
extracted in a day. The ironstone did not melt, but was
found at the bottom of the hearth in a large lump or
bloom, which was afterwards taken out and beaten under
massive hammers previous to its being worked into the
required shape or form."

The *burrs* found are the sand and iron mixed that
encased the *bloom*, which was taken out by pincers
and worked on the anvil. The scoria that encased
the bloom was thrown aside, and yet contains more
than one-half of iron. The iron reduced in this
simple manner never ran, but it became soft like
dough, and could be removed and beaten into
shape.

The method of dealing with the tin was similar,
only that in this latter case the metal flowed. That

foot bellows were employed before the system of
working bellows, and producing a continuous blast
by means of a water-wheel, is most probable. The
foot bellows are known to most primitive people,
but in Agricola's illustration of the smelting of tin

SLAG-POUNDING HOLLOWS, GOBBETTS.

none are shown. On the contrary, Æolus is represented in the corner as blowing a natural blast.

The book of Agricola, published in 1556, shows
that this primitive method was still in practice so
late as the middle of the sixteenth century.

But this clumsy method could not be long practised on Dartmoor, where fuel—except peat—was

I

scarce; and it gave way to a furnace of better construction, where the receiver was circular, and a draught-hole was at the bottom. One of these has

SMELTING ORE. (*After Agricola.*)

been dug out and carefully examined at Deep Swincombe.

It consists of a single chamber, 18 feet by 11 feet, rudely constructed of masses of granite resting on

PLAN OF BLOWING HOUSE, DEEP SWINCOMBE.

one another by their own weight and unset in mortar
or in clay.   The entrance was narrow and low.   On
one side was the furnace, constructed of granite, one
slab set upright to form a side, and the back and
other side built up rudely.   A fragment of the
receptacle for the molten tin was found, with a
receiver and channel cut in it.   Pottery was also
found, which was of a very early description.   It
was submitted to the late Sir Wollaston Franks, of
the British Museum, who said that he would have
attributed it to the Celtic period but for the bold
scores made at the starting-point of a handle, which
are characteristic of Anglo-Saxon pottery.

At the extremity furthest from the door was a
cache in the thickness of the wall, formed something
like a kistvaen, as a place in which to store the metal
and tools.   The whole structure was banked up with
rubble and turf.

Outside to the south still lies a mould-stone, a slab
of elvan, in which the mould had been cut, measuring
26 inches long by 12 inches at one end and 15 at the
other, and 5 inches deep.

That this is the earliest tin-furnace yet discovered
on Dartmoor admits of no doubt.   The curious mould-
stone is quite different in shape from any others
found on the moor.   No mortar - stones were discovered, and this also is a token of antiquity.

The earliest smelting arrangements must have
been very crude, and much tin was left in the slag.
Until recently the Malays threw away their slags,
which contained as much as 40 per cent. of tin.   As
there have been no mortar-stones found at Deep

Swincombe, it is to be presumed that the tinners disregarded their slags. These have not, moreover, been found. The reason was this—the sets had been reworked at a later time by the tinners at Gobbetts, further down the river. These later men had stone

TIN-MOULD, DEEP SWINCOMBE.

mortars and a crazing mill, and finding these rich slags, removed them, pounded them up in the hollowed mortar-stones, that may be seen *in situ* at Gobbetts, and resmelted them. Deep Swincombe has all the appearance of having been much pulled about by tinners since the first furnace was erected.

The tin running out of the furnace was allowed to flow into holes in the ground, and thence was ladled whilst in a molten condition and poured into the moulds.

Mr. Gowland has given a most interesting account of the manner in which the metals are extracted from their ores in Japan.* This shows how that the primitive methods are still in practice there. He says :—

"Although tin ore is found and worked in Japan in several localities, there is but one ancient mine in the country. It is situated in Taniyama, in the province of Satsuma. The excavations of the old miners here are of a most extensive character, the hillsides in places being literally honeycombed by their burrows, indicating the production in past times of large quantities of the metal. No remains, however, have been found to give any clue to the date of the earliest workings. But whatever may have been their date, the processes and appliances of the early smelters could not have been more primitive than those I found in use when I visited the mines in 1883.

"The ore was roughly broken up by hammers on stone anvils, then reduced to a coarse powder with the pounders used for decorticating rice, the mortars being large blocks of stone with roughly hollowed cavities.

"It was finally ground in stone querns, and washed by women in a stream to remove the earthy matter and foreign minerals with which it was contaminated. The furnace in which the ore was smelted is exactly the same as that used for copper ores, excepting that it is somewhat less in diameter. The ore was charged into it wet, in alternate layers with charcoal, and the process was conducted in precisely the same way as in smelting oxidised copper ores. The tin obtained was laded out of the furnace into moulds of clay."

* *Archæologia*, vol. lvi. part 2, 1899.

The furnace employed for copper is also described by Mr. Gowland :—

"An excavation, measuring about 4 feet long, 4 feet wide, and 2 feet deep, is made, and this is filled with dry clay carefully beaten down. In the centre of this bed of clay a shallow, conical-shaped hole is scooped out. The hole is

SMELTING TIN IN JAPAN.

then lined with a layer, about three inches thick, of damp clay mixed with charcoal, and the furnace is complete.

"It has no apertures either for the injection of the blast or for tapping out the metal. A blast of air is supplied to it generally from two bellows, placed behind a wall of wattle well coated with clay, by which they and the men working them are protected from the heat. The blast is led from each bellows by a bamboo tube, terminating in a very long nozzle of clay, which rests on the edge of the furnace cavity."

At Deep Swincombe no bellows were used ; the draught probably came in through the hole behind the furnace.

But in the reign of Queen Elizabeth a great revolution in the smelting of tin was wrought by the introduction of German workmen and their improved methods. They brought in the watèr-wheel. The ruins that are found in such abundance of "blowing-houses," as they are called—one at the least beside every considerable stream—belong, for the most part, to the Elizabethan period. They have their "leats" for carrying water to them, and their pits for tiny wheels that worked the bellows.

The situation of these smelting-houses may be found usually by the mould-stones that lie near them. There is one below the slide or fall of the Yealm, with its moulds in and by it, and another just above the fall. There is one near the megalithic remains at Drizzlecombe, also with its mould-stones. But it is unnecessary to particularise when they are so numerous. I will, however, quote Mr. R. Burnard's description of two in the Walkham valley as typical :

"The first is about 250 yards above Merrivale Bridge, on the left bank of the river. One jamb is erect, and, like most of the doorways of Dartmoor blowing-houses, was low, and to be entered necessitated an almost all-fours posture. Very little of the walls is standing, but what remains is composed of large moor-stones, dry laid. Near the entrance is a stone, 3 feet long and 2½ feet wide, containing a mould, which at the top is 18 inches long, 13 inches wide, and 6 inches deep. The sides are bevelled, so that the bottom length is 12½ inches, with a width of

7 inches at one end and 8 inches at the other. One end of the mould has a narrow gutter leading from the top to halfway down the mould. This was probably used for the insertion of a piece of iron prior to the metal being run in, thus permitting the easy withdrawal of the block of tin when cool from the mould. This stone also contains a small bevelled ingot or sample mould, 4 inches long, 2 inches wide, and $1\frac{1}{4}$ inches deep.

"A water-wheel probably stood in the eastern recess of the house, for there is a covered drain leading from here right under the house and out at the western end, where the water was discharged into the river. Traces of the leat which supplied the motive power to this wheel may also be seen.

"What appear to be the remains of the furnace, consisting of massive stones placed vertically, and inclosing a small rectangular space, are plainly visible. In this place, lying askew, as if it had been thrown out of position, is a large stone containing a long, shallow cavity, which may have been the bottom of the furnace or 'float,' *i.e.* the cavity in which the molten tin collected before being ladled into the mould.

"This ruin lies at the nether end of deep, open cuttings, which start from near Rundlestone Corner, and are continued right down to the Walkham.

"About 1,000 yards up stream is the ruin of the other blowing-house, with remains of a wheel-pit and a leat. There is also a stone containing a mould 16 inches long at the top, 11 inches wide, and 6 inches deep. It is bevelled, so that the bottom length is $12\frac{1}{2}$ inches, with a width of 8 inches. Like the mould-stone in the ruin below, it contains a sample ingot mould $3\frac{1}{2}$ inches long, 3 inches wide, and 2 inches deep. The remains in these ruins are very similar to each other, and these blowing-houses were probably smelting during the same period, indicating that a considerable quantity of tin was raised in their neighbourhood."*

Anciently, before the introduction of the wheel, the smelting-place above all others was at King's Oven, or Furnum Regis, near the Warren Inn, between Post Bridge and Moreton. It is mentioned in the *Perambulation of Dartmoor*, made in 1240. It consists of a circular inclosure of about seventy-two yards in diameter, forming a pound, with the remains of a quadrangular building in it. The furnace itself was destroyed some years ago. When the inclosure was made it was carried to a cairn that was in part demolished, to serve to form the bank of the pound. This cairn was ringed about with upright stones, and contained a kistvaen. The latter was rifled, and most of the stones removed to form the walls; but a few of the inclosing uprights were not meddled with, and between two was found firmly wedged a beautiful flint scraper.

As the drift tin was exhausted, and the slag of the earlier miners was used up, it became necessary to run adits for tin, and work the veins. These adits remain in several places, and where they have been opened have yielded up iron bars and picks. But these are not more ancient than mediæval times, probably late in them. That gold was found in the granite rubble of the stream-beds is likely. A model of a gold-washing apparatus was found on the moor a few years ago. It was made of zinc.

* *Dartmoor Pictorial Records*, 1893.

According to an old Irish historical narrative, a bard was wont to carry a wand of "white bronze" or tin, and his shoes were also tin-plated.* One wonders whether at any time a bard thus shod and with his rod of office strode over Dartmoor and chanted historic ballads there!

For such as would care to see these dry bones of antiquarian research into the past of tin-streamers clothed with flesh, I must refer them to my novel of *Guavas the Tinner*, in which I have described the mode of life of the metal-seekers on the moor in the time of Elizabeth.

* *Silva Gadhelica*, ii. p. 271.

CHAPTER IX.

LYDFORD

An out-of-the-world spot—The church dilapidated—The clerk—
Situation of Lydford—An early fortress—The church of S. Petrock
—British foundations—Monument of the watchmaker—The castle
—A prison—Mr. Radford—Will Huggins—Primitive gate-hinges—
The gorge—The waterfall—The Gubbins crew—Black Down—
Entries in the registers of Mary Tavy—Mary and Peter Tavy
churches—Bridestowe church—Bronescombe's Loaf and Cheese
—Tavy Cleave—Peat-works—Cross on Sourton Down.

FIFTY years ago Lydford was one of the most
out-of-the-world and wild spots in England.
I had almost written God-forsaken, but checked my
pen, for God forsakes no place, though He may tarry
to bless. There were no resident gentry—there never
had been, as a glance at the registers reveals. There
was no resident rector—there had not been within
the memory of the oldest inhabitant. The rector
was a wealthy ‚pluralist, rector of Southill and
Callington, in Cornwall, who hardly ever showed his
face in Lydford, the largest parish in England, and
maintained a poor curate there on a hundred pounds
a year in a miserable cottage.

The people were a law to themselves, and had the
credit of being inveterate poachers.

The houses, thatched, built of moor-stones, not set
in mortar, were in a ruinous condition. The aspect

ON THE LYD

of the place was that of an Irish village. It was dominated by a ruined castle, and possessed a church fast lapsing to ruin, and was girt in by walls long ago reduced to heaps. One Christmas Day the curate went to the church for the celebration of the Holy Communion, and found the altar covered with snow that had blown in through the battered east window and under the cracked slates of the roof.

" I'll sweep it off," said the clerk.

" On no account. God has spread His table," said the curate ; and he celebrated on the white sheet of snow.

In the cottage that served as parsonage it was not much better. The curate had two rooms downstairs and one above. One room was slate-paved. Up-stairs there was no ceiling, and he had occasionally to spread his umbrella over his head and pillow when he went to bed.

Now all is changed, or changing.

The church has been restored, and is a model of what a church should be. The old parsonage has been pulled down, and stables built on the site, and the late Mr. Street, the architect, erected an absurd Scottish castle with angle turrets and extinguisher caps to serve as rectory. The ruinous houses are being replaced by trim, if ugly, habitations. Only the gaunt castle remains gutted.

About fifty years ago the clerk was addicted to lifting his elbow too freely, and came to church occa-sionally in a hilarious condition. The climax was reached at a funeral, when he tumbled into the grave before the coffin, and apostrophised the dead man as he scrambled out: "Beg parding, Ted; I bain't minded to change places wi' you just yet."

The curate was compelled to discharge him and appoint another, Peter X.

The old clerk refused to accept his dismissal, and gathered his adherents, and on the ensuing Sunday marched at their head to the house of God. Peter, advised of this, summoned his supporters, and, having the keys, ensconced himself early within the sacred building, in the clerk's pew, surrounded by his upholders. The rival party entered, and a battle ensued between the factions. The curate absolutely refused to perform the service to the clerking of the dismissed official, and finally the latter and his gang were ejected from the church, loudly professing that they would all turn Dissenters.

This Peter remained clerk for fifty years. He obtained a subsidiary revenue by carrying children afflicted with "the thrush" up the tower, and holding them over the battlements at each pinnacle, whilst he recited the Lord's Prayer. For this he received a small gratuity.

He was a most worthy man, and, as he is now dead, I do not scruple to mention that the story I have told in *Furze Bloom*, under the title of "Peter Lempole," pertained to him. He never married, the reason being that he had a childish old brother entirely dependent on him. Peter was engaged to a bright, pretty girl; but one day she said to him, "When us is married, then, mind y', Peter, I'm not going to have that silly brother of yourn in the house with me." "Indeed!" was Peter's retort; "then into my house *you* shall never come."

Lydford occupies a tongue of land between two ravines, one cleft perpendicularly to a depth of seventy feet, the other steep, but not sheer through rock. The old line of fortifications, much degraded by the plough, may be traced distinctly, nevertheless, across the only portion of the headland by which attack was possible. It is the sort of fortress which goes by the name of cliff castle on the Cornish and Welsh coasts.

That it was a site chosen by the prehistoric population is undoubted. Such a natural fortress could not have been overlooked, and it was held since remote times till the Normans came. Yet, notwithstanding the position being almost impregnable, it was taken, and the town of Lydford was burnt by the Danes in 997 after they had destroyed the Abbey of Tavistock. From Domesday it would appear that at the Conquest Lydford was a walled town. It sent burgesses to Parliament twice in the reign of Edward I.

The church is dedicated to S. Petrock, and at its restoration some remains of the old British church were discovered three feet below the pavement of the present edifice. The slabs that had lain on the floor of the original oratory were taken up and placed within the doorway of the present church; so that the worshippers may stand on the very stones on which their ancestors stood in the sixth century. That into the walls of the reconstructed church most of the stones of the original edifice were incorporated, is more than probable.

There are several Petrock churches round the moor

—Harford, South Brent, Clannaborough ; and probably the original founder and patron of Buckfast Abbey was this saint.

The great distinction between British foundations and those that were Roman was this: a British church was called after its founder, whereas a Roman church received its name from some scraps of dead bones of a saint laid under the altar, or placed in it. Unhappily, we have no record of S. Petrock's labours in Devon, but there can exist little hesitation in holding that he was an apostle of the district about Dartmoor and of a tract north of it as well, as also that he laboured and died in Cornwall.

Here is what Bede tells us of the manner of consecration among the Celts. It must be premised that the historian is speaking of Cedd, Bishop of the East Saxons from 653 to 664, to whom Oidilvald, King of the Deisa, had given a piece of land. Cedd had received his training from Celtic monks at Iona.

"This man of God, wishing by prayer and fasting to purge the place of its former pollution of wickedness, and so to lay the foundation of the monastery, entreated the king that he would grant him the means and permission to dwell there for that purpose, during the whole time of Lent, which was then at hand. In all the days of this time, except on Sundays, he fasted till the evening, according to custom, and then took no other sustenance than a little bread, one hen's egg, and a little milk mixed with water. This, he said, was the custom of those of whom he had learned the rule of regular discipline ; first to consecrate to our Lord, by prayer and fasting, the places which they had newly received for building a monastery or a church.

"When there were ten days of Lent still remaining there came a messenger to call him to the king, and he, that the religious work might not be intermitted, on account of the king's affairs, entreated his priest, Cynebil, who was also his brother, to complete the work that had been so piously begun. Cynebil readily complied, and when the time of fasting and prayer was over he there built the monastery, which is now called Lastingham." *

The name Petrock is really Peterkin, the Celtic diminutive of Peter, and it is probable that Peter Tavy is another of his foundations, as well as certain other churches now regarded as dedicated to the great apostle.

The Saxons, who were saturated with Latin ideas, when they obtained supremacy, rededicated the churches to saints of the Roman calendar, if they were able to obtain from Italy some scraps of bone that it was pretended had belonged to one of the saints of the Latin calendar. But there is no evidence that the British Christians did other than call their churches after the names of the founders.

Lydford church is of fifteenth-century Perpendicular, but in the chancel is an earlier piscina, and the font is possibly pre-Norman. The chancel screen is gone, but the rood staircase remains.

In the churchyard is the often-quoted epitaph of George Routleigh :—

"Here lies in horizontal position
the outside case of
George Routleigh, watch-maker,

* *Hist. Eccl.*, iii. c. 23.

K

whose abilities in that line were an honour
to his profession.
Integrity was the main-spring
and Prudence the regulator
of all the actions of his life.
Humane, generous and liberal
his Hand never stopped
till he had relieved distress.
So nicely regulated were all his motions
that he never went wrong,
except when set agoing
by people who did not know his key.
Even then he was easily set right again.
He had the art of disposing his time so well
that his hours glided away
in one continual round
of pleasure and delight.
Till an unlucky minute put a period to
his existence.
He departed this life Nov. 14, 1802,
aged 57,
wound up
in hopes of being taken in hand
by his Maker
and of being thoroughly cleaned, repaired
and set agoing
in the World to Come."

In the churchyard may be noticed some altar
tombs of the type not infrequent round the moor.

Due west of the church, across the graveyard
hedge, is a small camp, possibly British.

The castle is planted on a tump, a natural elevation artificially shaped, and is not particularly interesting. It is square, and was built after the Conquest.

By a charter of Edward I. it was constituted a Stannary prison. Richard Strode, of Newnham Park, one of the principal gentry of the county, moved in Parliament to restrain the miners from discharging their refuse into the rivers with the result of choking up the harbours. The miners were so incensed against him that they captured him in 1512, had him summarily tried by their Stannary Laws, on Crockern Tor, and threw him into Lydford gaol, where he languished for some time, and it was with considerable difficulty that his release was obtained.

What with Forest Laws and Stannary Laws, Lydford Castle rarely lacked tenants. Even in 1399 Lydford law was held in bad repute, for Wright, in his collection of political poems, prints some verses of that date which speak of it as such; and William Browne, in 1644, wrote on it :—

> " I oft have heard of Lydford law,
>   How in the morn they hang and draw,
>   And sit in judgment after :
>   At first I wondered at it much,
>   But soon I found the matter such
>   As it deserves no laughter.

> " They have a castle on a hill ;
>   I took it for some old wind-mill,
>   The vanes blown off by weather.
>   Than lie therein one night 'tis guessed
>   'Twere better to be stoned or pressed
>   Or hanged, ere you come thither."

And so on for sixteen verses.

Below the castle is the water-gate where is the only spring from which Lydford town was supplied till Mr. Radford brought drinking water into the place.

With Lydford the name of Daniel Radford will be indissolubly connected—one of the noblest and kindest of men, and one of the most modest. He cut the way up the ravine by which the gorge was made accessible. When I was a boy the only method by which it could be explored was by swimming and scrambling in summer, when the water was low. Mr. Radford built Bridge House and restored the church. It was due to him that I undertook, in 1888, to collect the folk-music in Devon and Cornwall; and it is in Lydford churchyard that he lies, awaiting the resurrection of the just. Not without deep feeling can I pen these lines to commemorate one of the best men whom it has been my happiness to know.

As I have mentioned the folk-music of Devon, I may here add that one of my assistants was old Will Huggins, of Lydford, a mason, who entered enthusiastically into the work. I had an attack of influenza in the winter of 1889–90, and had to leave England for Italy. Before my departure Will promised me to go about among his old cronies and collect ancient ballads. Alas! he caught a chill; it fell on his chest, and when I returned in the spring, it was to learn that he was gone.

> " I'm going, I reckon, full mellow
>   To lay in the churchyard my head ;
> So say, God be wi' you, old fellow,
>   The last of the singers is dead."

In the village street may be noticed, built into the hedge or wall, a piece of granite with a round hole like a rock basin depressed in it. Actually it is one of the stones of a gate-hinge.

Formerly the gates around Dartmoor had no iron hinges, but turned in sockets cut in granite blocks. Few of these now remain in use, but the stones may be noticed lying about in many places, and it is really

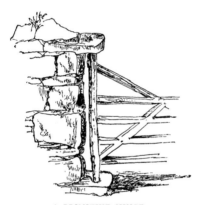

A PRIMITIVE HINGE.

marvellous that the antiquaries of the past did not suppose they were basins for sacrificial lustration.

In 1880 the late Mr. Lukis was in Devon, planning the rude stone monuments on Dartmoor for the Royal Society of Antiquaries. He came on some of these cuplike holes in stones, and carefully measured and drew them. Happily, I was able to show a gate swinging between two of these blocks, and so explain to him their purpose.

The Lydford ravine is the finest of its kind in England. A bridge crosses it, and it is worth while looking over the parapet into the gulf below, through which the river writhes and leaps. The gardens of Bridge House are thrown open on Mondays, when a visitor may descend and thread the gorge. But decidedly the best way for him to see the beauties of the Lyd valley, where most restricted and romantic, is for him to descend at the waterfall, a pretty but not grand slide of a lateral brook, and ascend the ravine of the Lyd from thence; he will pass through the gorge where finest, under the bridge, and pursue his course till he comes out at a mill below the south gate of Lydford. Hence a half-mile will take him to Kitt's Steps, another fall, a leap of the Lyd into a basin half choked with the rubbish from a mine. The mine happily failed, but it has left its heaps in the glen as a permanent disfigurement.

Considerable caution must be exercised in ascending the gorge, as the path is narrow, and in places slippery. A schoolmistress was killed here a few years ago. She turned to look at the sun glancing through the leaves at the entrance of the chasm, became giddy, and fell over. She was dead when her body was recovered.

Inhabiting the valley and lateral combes of the Lyd, in the time of Charles I. and the Commonwealth, was a race of men called the Gubbinses. They were wild and lawless, and maintained themselves by stealing sheep and cattle, and carrying them into the labyrinth of glens where they could not be traced.

Fuller, in his account of the wonders of the county of Devon, includes the Gubbinses. He heard of them during his stay in Exeter, 1644-7.

"I have read of an England beyond Wales, but the Gubbings land is a Scythia within England, and they be pure heathens therein. It lyeth near Brenttor, in the edge of Dartmore. . . . They are a peculiar of their own making, exempt from Bishop, Archdeacon, and all Authority, either ecclesiastical or civil. They live in cotts (rather holes than houses) like swine, having all in common, multiplied, without marriage, into many hundreds. Their language is the drosse of the dregs of the vulgar Devonian ; and the more learned a man is, the worse he can understand them. Their wealth consists in other men's goods, and they live by stealing the sheep on the More, and vain it is for any to search their Houses, being a Work beneath the pains of a Sheriff, and above the powers of any constable. Such their fleetness, they will out-run many horses : vivaciousnesse, they outlive most men, living in the ignorance of luxury, the Extinguisher of Life, they hold together like Burrs, offend One, and All will revenge his quarrel."

William Browne speaks of them as near Lydford :—

> "And near thereto's the Gubbins' cave,
> A people that no knowledge have
>   Of law, of God, or men ;
> Whom Cæsar never yet subdued ;
> Who've lawless liv'd ; of manners rude ;
>   All savage in their den.

> " By whom, if any pass that way,
> He dares not the least time to stay,
>   But presently they howl ;
> Upon which signal they do muster
> Their naked forces in a cluster,
>   Led forth by Roger Rowle."

It cannot be said that the race is altogether extinct. The magistrates have had much trouble with certain persons living in hovels on the outskirts of the moor, who subsist in the same manner. They carry off lambs and young horses before they are marked, and when it is difficult, not to say impossible, for the owners to identify them. Their own ewes always have doubles.

In the West Okement valley, in a solitary spot, are the foundations of a cottage in which for many years a man lived, preying upon the flocks and cattle on the moor, and carrying on his depredations with such cunning that he was never caught. It was shrewdly suspected that he was in league with a number of small farmers, and that he was by this means able to pass on his captures and ensure their concealment.

Black Down is an extensive ridge of moorland traversed by the high road from Okehampton to Tavistock. The highest point is called Gibbet Hill, but tradition is silent as to who hung there.

In the Mary Tavy register occurs this entry :—

"1691, March 12, William Warden, a currier, was whipped by the Parson and Churchwardens of Whitchurch, and ordered to be passed on as a wandering rogue from parish to parish, by the officers therein, in 26 days to his native place, Cheshunt in Hertfordshire, and as the Churchwardens were conveying him on horseback over Black Down, he died on the back of the horse, and was buried the same night."

The parson of Whitchurch was a Mr. Polwhele, who was also justice of peace.

Here is another curious entry in the same book of registers :—

"1756, Sept. 12, Robert Elford, was baptized, the child of Susanna Elford by her sister's husband, to whom she was married with the consent of her sister, the wife, who was at the wedding."

Here the union is not with a *deceased* wife's sister, but the living wife's sister. There is no entry relative to this marriage, so that the pair must have got their unhallowed union blessed in some remote parish, where the relationship was not known.

In 1760 William Creedy, sojourner, and Susanna Elford had their banns called, but there is no entry of a marriage.

Another entry in the same register book is suggestive of a scandal.

"1627, Aug. 5, Baptized, Nicolas filius Mri. Johan. Cake jam senio confecti."

Mary Tavy church, picturesquely situated, not on the Tavy, but on a little confluent, was barbarously renovated some years ago, but of late much loving care has been bestowed upon the structure, and something has been done to efface the mischief wrought by the architect who had dealt with it previously. The new screen is remarkably good, and in accordance with Devonshire work of the sixteenth century. The stained glass is excellent.

Peter Tavy church was disfigured rather later than Mary Tavy. It possessed an interesting Tudor square pew, richly carved, and with posts at the

corners supporting heraldic beasts. This was demolished at the so-called restoration. Some scraps
have been preserved and worked up to form a screen
across the tower arch. All the modern work is of
the vulgarest description, in yellow deal. A portion
of the screen with saints painted on it is preserved
within the altar rails.

Peter Tavy Combe must on no account be
neglected; it is a remarkably picturesque valley.

Another church that may be visited from Lydford
is Bridestowe, dedicated to S. Bridget, who had a
sanctuary of refuge here, now called the Sentry.
The original church stood in a different position,
and contained the Norman arch now erected at the
entrance to the church avenue. It was turned into
a church-house, then became ruinous and was pulled
down. The reason for the removal of the parish
church in the fifteenth century was probably because
the old church was near the road at a turn, so that
there was not space available to enlarge it.

This church has suffered from maltreatment by
a late rector, who tore down the old roodscreen,
sawed it down the middle, and plastered the tracery
so treated against a deal dwarf screen, *inverted*,
and against a vestry door. To make matters worse,
he boarded the entire interior of the chancel with
deal, varnished. It presented the appearance of a
cabin of a ship. This has now happily disappeared.
It is greatly to be desired that the screen should
be restored.

Second to the Dart only in beauty is the West
Okement that comes foaming down from the bogs

about Cranmere through a fine ravine between Yes Tor and Amicombe Hill. If the river be followed up from Meldon Viaduct, a point is reached where it rushes over a barrier-of rocks fallen from Black Tor, and divides about an islet. But perhaps the best way to see this valley is to ascend a combe, crossed at the foot by the Lake Viaduct, and follow a track that sweeps round Sourton Tor, and ascend to Bronescombe's Loaf and Cheese, where is a fine cairn. On the slope between Sourton Tor and Bronescombe's Loaf lies a large slab of granite through which a dyke of elvan has been thrust. In this elvan have been cut the moulds for two bronze axe-heads.

Walter Bronescombe was Bishop of Exeter between 1258 and 1280, and he lies buried in the Cathedral under a fine canopied tomb. The effigy is of his own date, and gives apparently a true portrait of a worthy prelate.

One day he was visiting this portion of his diocese, and had ventured to ride over the moor from Widdecombe. He and his retinue had laboured through bogs, and almost despaired of reaching the confines of the wilderness. Moreover, on attaining Amicombe Hill they knew not which way to take, for the bogs there are nasty ; and his attendants dispersed to seek a way. The Bishop was overcome with fatigue, and was starving. He turned to his chaplain and said, " Our Master in the wilderness was offered by Satan bread made of stones. If he were now to make the same offer to me, I doubt if I should have the Christian fortitude to refuse."

"Ah!" sighed the chaplain, "and a hunch of cheese as well!"

"Bread and cheese I could not hold out against," said the Bishop.

Hardly had he spoken before a moorman rose up from a peat dyke and drew nigh; he had a wallet on his back.

"Master!" called the chaplain, "dost thou chance to have a snack of meat with thee?"

"Ay, verily," replied the moorman, and approached, hobbling, for he was apparently lame. "I have with me bread and cheese, naught else."

"Give it us, my son," said the Bishop; "I will well repay thee."

"Nay," replied the stranger, "I be no son of thine. And I ask no reward save that thou descend from thy steed, doff thy cap, and salute me with the title of master."

"I will do that," said the Bishop, and alighted.

Then the strange man produced a loaf and a large piece of cheese.

Now, the Bishop was about to take off his cap and address the moorman in a tone of entreaty and by the title of master, when the chaplain perceived that the man had one foot like that of a goat. He instantly cried out to God, and signified what he saw to the prelate, who, in holy horror, made the sign of the cross, and lo! the moorman vanished, and the bread and cheese remained transformed to stone.

Do you doubt it? Go and see. Look on the Ordnance Survey map and you will find Bread

HARE TOR

and Cheese marked there.   Only Bronescombe's
name has been transformed to Brandescombe.

But the Bishop, to make atonement, and to
ease his conscience for having so nearly yielded
to temptation, spent great sums on the rebuilding
of his cathedral.

From the Bread and Cheese, a walk along the
brow of the hill by the Slipper Stones—so called
because there Bishop Bronescombe dropped one
of the coverings of his feet—shows the valley to
perfection, with Black Tor rising above it, and Yes
Tor towering high aloft in the rear.   By the stream
below is a stunted copse, a relic of the ancient arms
of forest that stole up the ravines far into the moor,
but of which now hardly any remain.   At Stinga
Tor, further up, is a fine logan rock.   The visitor
may return by the peat-works and the noble pile of
Lynx Tor to the valley of the Lyd.

An interesting excursion may be made to Tavy
Cleave.   The course to be adopted, so as to see it in
perfection, is to go on to the moor from the Dartmoor
Inn.   Here in its proper season, August to October,
the field gentian, with its dull purple flowers, may be
gathered.   A descent to the Lyd by some old mine
works opens a fine view of Lynx, Hare, and Doe
Tors, and the little farm named after the latter lies
before one, solitary in the midst of heather and
swamp.   Stepping-stones allow the river to be
crossed, and the farm is reached and passed, and
Hare Tor is aimed at.   Old stream-works and pro-
specting pits abound.   By leaving the summit of
Hare Tor on the left, a cluster of rocks rising above

the grass and heather must be struck at, and suddenly before the eye opens the ravine of the Tavy, that foams far below over a bar of red granite.

Between the rocks and Ger Tor is a cluster of hut circles in tolerable preservation, and a very interesting collection is found on a spur of Stannon, on the further side of the Tavy.

Lynx Tor may be ascended from Lydford. The summit is occupied by a fine mass of rocks, and

INSCRIPTION ON SOURTON CROSS.

commands a superb view as far as the Atlantic in one direction, and Plymouth Sound and the Channel in another.

Near Lynx Tor are the peat-works already mentioned. Various attempts have been made to find for the peat a use that may prove commercially successful, but hitherto these attempts have not been satisfactory to investors. The bogs are hungry, and swallow up a good deal of money.

Hence a short diversion will take to the logan rock on Stinga Tor.

On Sourton Down stands an old granite cross that

bears an inscription only to be read when the sun is setting and casts its rays aslant over the face. Apparently the monolith was shaped into a Latin cross at some period later than the inscription, which belongs to the sixth century. It is headed by the early Christian symbol of the ☧, but badly made. The same symbol occurs on the inscribed stone at Southill. The granite is of a very coarse texture, especially where the figure occurs and at the beginning of the name.

As for every person, so for every place, a time comes if waited for. It has come for Lydford, burnt by Danes, deserted in the Middle Ages, abandoned by its rectors.

> "At six o'clock I came along
> And prayed for those that were to stay
> Within a place so arrant ;
> Wide and ope the winds so roar,
> By God's grace I'll come there no more
> Till forc'd by a tin warrant."

So wrote Browne in the seventeenth century.

But the time has arrived for Lydford at last, and now in summer it is hardly possible for a visitor to obtain lodgings, unless he has written to secure them months before, so greatly does Lydford attract to it those who have eyes to see beautiful scenery and hearts to appreciate it.

CHAPTER X.

BELSTONE

Derivation of the name—Phœnicians—Taw Marsh—Artillery practice on the moors—Encroachments—The East Okement—Pounds and hut circles—Stone rows on Cosdon—Cranmere Pool—Sticklepath —Christian inscribed stones—South Zeal—West Wyke—North Wyke—The wicked Richard Weekes—South Tawton church—The West Okement—Yes Tor—Camp and Roman road—Throwleigh.

A GOOD deal of pseudo-antiquarianism has been expressed relative to the name of a little moorland parish two and a half miles uphill from Okehampton. It is now called Belstone, and it has been surmised that here stood a stone dedicated to Baal, whose worship had been introduced by the Phœnicians.

I must really quote one of the finest specimens of "exquisite fooling" I have ever come across. It appeared as a sub-article in the *Western Morning News* in 1890.

It was headed :—

"PHŒNICIANS IN DART VALE.

"[SPECIAL.]

"Much interest, not only local but world-wide, was aroused a few months back by the announcement of a Phœnician survival at Ipplepen, in the person of Mr. Thomas Ballhatchet, descendant of the priest of the Sun

Temple there, and until lately owner of the plot of land called Baalford, under Baal Tor, a priestly patrimony, which had come down to him through some eighteen or twenty centuries, together with his name and his marked Levantine features and characteristics.

"Such survivals are not infrequent among Orientals, as, for instance, the Cohens, Aaron's family, the Bengal Brahmins, the Rechabites, etc. Ballhatchet's sole peculiarity is his holding on to the land, in which, however, he is kept in countenance in England by the Purkises, who drew the body of Rufus to its grave in Winchester Cathedral on 2nd August, 1100.

" Further quiet research makes it clear beyond all manner of doubt that the Phœnician tin colony, domiciled at Totnes, and whose Sun Temple was located on their eastern sky-line at Ipplepen, have left extensive traces of their presence all the way down the Dart in the identical and unaltered names of places, a test of which the Palestine Exploration Committee record the priceless value. To give but one instance. The beautiful light-refracting diadem which makes Belliver* the most striking of all her sister tors, received from the Semite its consecration as 'Baallivyah,' Baal, crown of beauty or glory. The word itself occurs in Proverbs i. 9 and iv. 9, and as both Septuagint and Vulgate so render it, it must háve borne that meaning in the third century B.C., and in the third century A.D., and, of course, in the interval. There are many other instances quite as close, and any student of the new and fascinating science of Assyriology will continually add to them. A portrait of Ballhatchet, with some notes by an eminent and well-known Semitic scholar, may probably appear in the *Graphic;* in the meantime it may be pointed out that his

* Belliver is a modern contraction of Bellaford, as Redever is Redaford.

L

name is typically Babylonian. Not only is there at Pantellaria the gravestone of one Baal-yachi (Baal's beloved), but no less than three clay tablets from the Sun Temple of Sippara (the Bible Sepharvaim) bear the names of Baal-achi-iddin, Baal-achi-utsur, and Baal-achi-irriba. This last, which bears date *22* Sivan (in the eleventh year of Nabonidus, B.C. 540), just two years before the catastrophe which followed on Belshazzar's feast, is in the possession of Mr. W. G. Thorpe, F.S.A. It is in beautiful condition, and records a loan by one Dinkiva to Baal-achi-irriba (Baal will protect his brother), on the security of some slaves."

One really wonders in reading such nonsense as this whether modern education is worth much, when a man could write such trash and an editor could admit it into his paper.

Ballhatchet means the hatchet or gate to a ball, *i.e.* a mine.

As it happens, there is not a particle of trustworthy evidence that the Phœnicians ever traded directly with Cornwall and Devon. The intermediary traders were the Veneti of what is now Vannes, and the tin trade was carried through Gaul to Marseilles, as is shown by traces left on the old trade route. In the next place, there is no evidence that our British or Ivernian ancestors ever heard the name of Baal. And finally, Belstone is not named after a stone at all, to return to the point whence we started. In Domesday it is Bellestham, or the *ham*, meadow of Belles or Bioll, a Saxon name that remains among us as Beale.

Belstone is situated at the lip of Taw Marsh, once a fine lake, with Steeperton Tor rising above it at the head. Partly because the river has fretted a way through the joints of the granite, forming Belstone Cleave, and partly on account of the silting up of the lake-bed with rubble brought down by the several streams that here unite, the lake-bed is now filled up with sand and gravel and swamp.

The military authorities coveted this tract for artillery practice. They set up butts, but woman intervened. A very determined lady marched up to them, although the warning red flags fluttered, and planted herself in front of a target, took out of her reticule a packet of ham sandwiches and a flask of cold tea, and declared her intention of spending the day there. In vain did the military protest, entreat, remonstrate; she proceeded to nibble at her sandwiches and defied them to fire.

She carried the day.

Since then Taw Marsh has been the playfield of many children, and has been rambled over by visitors, but the artillery have abstained from practising on it.

The fact is that the military have made the moors about Okehampton impossible for the visitor, and those who desire to rove over it in pursuit of health have been driven from Okehampton to Belstone, and object to be moved on further.

What with the camp at Okehampton and the prisons at Princetown and encroachments on every side, the amount of moorland left open to the rambler is greatly curtailed.

The privation is not only felt by the visitor but also by the farmer, who has a right to send out his sheep and cattle upon the moor in summer, and in times of drought looks to this upland as his salvation.

A comparison between what the Forest of Dartmoor was at the beginning of this century and its condition to-day shows how inclosures have crept on—nay, not crept, increased by leaps; and what is true of the forest is true also of the commons that surround it. Add to the inclosed land the large tract swept by the guns at Okehampton, and the case becomes more grave still. The public have been robbed of their rights wholesale. Not a word can now be raised against the military. The Transvaal War has brought home to us the need we have to become expert marksmen, and the Forest of Dartmoor seems to offer itself for the purpose of a practising-ground. Nevertheless, one accepts the situation with a sigh.

There is a charming excursion up the East Okement from the railway bridge to Cullever Steps, passing on the way a little fall of the river, not remarkable for height but for picturesqueness. There is no path, and the excursion demands exertion.

On Belstone Common is a stone circle and near it a fallen menhir. The circle is merely one of stones that formed a hut, which had upright slabs lining it within as well as girdling without.

Under Belstone Tor, among the "old men's workings" by the Taw, an experienced eye will detect a blowing-house, but it is much dilapidated.

The Taw and an affluent pour down from the central bog, one on each side of Steeperton Tor,

and from the east the small brook dances into Taw
Marsh. Beside the latter, on the slopes, are numerous pounds and hut circles, and near its source is
a stone circle, of which the best uprights have
been carried off for gateposts. South of it is a
menhir, the Whitmoor Stone, leaning, as the
ground about it is marshy. Cosdon, or, as it is
incorrectly called occasionally, Cawsand, is a huge
rounded hill ascending to 1,785 feet, crowned with
dilapidated cairns and ruined kistvaens. East of the
summit, near the turf track from South Zeal, is a
cairn that contained three kistvaens. One is perfect,
one wrecked, and of the third only the space remained and indications whence the slabs had been
torn. From these three kistvaens in one mound
start three stone rows that are broken through by
the track, but can be traced beyond it for some
way ; they have been robbed, as the householders of
South Zeal have been of late freely inclosing large
tracts of their common, and have taken the stones
for the construction of walls about their fields.

By ascending the Taw, Cranmere Pool may be
reached, but is only so far worth the visit that the
walk to and from it gives a good insight into the
nature of the central bogs. The pool is hardly more
than a puddle. Belstone church is not interesting ;
it was rebuilt, all but the tower, in 1881.

Under Cosdon nestles Sticklepath. " Stickle " is the
Devonshire for steep. Here is a holy well near an
inscribed stone. A second inscribed stone is by the
roadside to Okehampton. At Belstone are two more,
but none of these bear names. They are Chris-

tian monuments of the sixth, or at latest seventh, century. At Sticklepath was a curious old cob thatched chapel, but this has been unnecessarily destroyed, and a modern erection of no interest or

INSCRIBED STONE, STICKLEPATH.

beauty has taken its place. South Zeal is an in-teresting little village, through which ran the old high-road, but which is now left on one side. For long it was a treasury of interesting old houses; many have disappeared recently, but the "Oxenham Arms," the seat of the Burgoyne family, remains, the fine old village cross, and the chapel, of granite.

Above South Zeal, on West Wyke Moor, is the house that belonged to the Battishill family, with a ruined cross near it. The house has been much spoiled of late; the stone mullions have been removed from the hall window, but the ancient gateway, surmounted by the Battishill arms, and with the date 1656, remains untouched. It is curious, because one would hardly have expected a country gentleman to have erected an embattled gateway during the Commonwealth, and in the style of the early Tudor kings. In the hall window are the arms of Battishill, impaled with a coat that cannot be determined as belonging to any known family. In the same parish of South Tawton is another old house, North Wyke, that belonged to the Wyke or Weekes family. The ancient gatehouse and chapel are interesting; they belong, in my opinion, to the sixteenth century, and to the latter part of the same. The chapel has a corbel, the arms of Wykes and Gifford; and John Wyke of North Wyke, who was buried in 1591, married the daughter of Sir Roger Gifford. The gateway can hardly be earlier. The house was built by the same man, but underwent great alteration in the fashion introduced from France by Charles II., when the rooms were raised and the windows altered into *croisées*.

Touching this house a tale is told.

About the year 1660 there was a John Weekes of North Wyke, who was a bachelor, and lived in the old mansion along with his sister Katherine, who was unmarried, and his mother. He was a man

of weak intellect, and was consumptive. John came
of age in 1658. In the event of his death without
will his heir would be his uncle John, his father's
brother, who died in 1680. This latter John had
a son Roger.

Now it happened that there was a great scamp
of the name of Richard Weekes, born at Hatherleigh,
son of Francis Weekes of Honeychurch, possibly a
remote connection, but not demonstrably so.

He was a gentleman pensioner of Charles II., but
spent most of his leisure time in the Fleet Prison.
One day this rascal came down from London, it
is probable at the suggestion of consumptive John's
mother and sister, who could not be sure what he,
with his feeble mind, might do with the estate.

Richard ingratiated himself into the favour of
John, and urged him not to risk his health in so
bleak and exposed a spot as South Tawton, but
to seek a warmer climate, and he invited him to
Plymouth. The unsuspicious John assented.

When John was cajoled to Plymouth, Richard
surrounded him with creatures of his own, a doctor
and two lawyers, who, with Richard's assistance,
coaxed, bullied, and persuaded the sickly John into
making a deed of settlement of all his estate in
favour of Richard. The unhappy man did this, but
with a curious proviso enabling him to revoke his
act by word as well as by deed. Richard had now
completely outwitted John's mother and sister, who
had been conspirators with him, on the understanding
that they were to share the spoils.

After a while, when it was clear that John was

NORTH WYKE GATE HOUSE

dying, Richard hurried him back to North Wyke, where he expired on Saturday, September 21st, 1661, but not till he had been induced by his mother and sister to revoke his will verbally, for they had now learned how that the wily Richard had got the better of them.

Next day, Sunday, Richard Weekes arrived, booted and spurred, at the head of a party of men he had collected. With sword drawn he burst into the house, and when Katherine Weekes attempted to bar the way he knocked her down. Then he drove the widow mother into a closet and locked the door on her. He now cleared the house of the servants, and proceeded to take possession of all the documents and valuables that the mansion contained. Poor John's body lay upstairs : no regard was paid to that, and, saying " I am come to do the devil's work and my own," he drove Katherine out of the house, and she was constrained to take refuge for the night in a neighbouring farm. The widow, Mary Weekes, was then liberated and also turned out of doors.

The heir-at-law was the uncle John, against whom Mary and Katherine Weekes had conspired with the scoundrel Richard. This latter now sought Uncle John, made him drunk, and got him to sign a deed, when tipsy, conveying all his rights to the said Richard for the sum of fifty pounds paid down. Richard was now in possession. The widow thereupon brought an action in Chancery against Richard. The lawyers saw the opportunity. Here was a noble estate that might be sucked dry, and they descended on it with this end in view.

The lawsuit was protracted for forty years, from 1661 to 1701, when the heirs of the wicked Richard retained the property, but it had been so exhausted and burdened, that the suit was abandoned undecided. Richard Weekes died in 1670.

The plan resorted to in order to keep possession after the forcible entry was this. The son of Richard Weekes had married a Northmore of Well, in South Tawton, and the Northmores bought up all the debts on the estate and got possession of the mortgages, and worked them persistently and successfully against the rightful claimants till, worried and wearied out, and with empty purses, they were unable further to pursue the claim. In 1713 the estate was sold by John Weekes, the grandson of Richard, who had also married a Northmore, and North Wyke passed away from the family after having been in its possession since the reign of Henry III.

It was broken up into two farms, and the house divided into two. Recently it has, however, been repurchased by a descendant of the original possessors, in a female line, the Rev. W. Wykes Finch, and the house is being restored in excellent taste.

In South Tawton church is a fine monument of the common ancestor, John Wyke, 1591. The church has been renovated, monumental slabs sawn in half and used to line the drain round the church externally. With the exception of the sun-dial, bearing the motto from Juvenal, " *Obrepet non intellecta senectus*," and a Burgoyne monument and that of " Warrior Wyke," the church does not present much of interest at present, whatever it may have done before it fell into the hands of spoilers.

The West Okement comes down from the central bogs through a fine "Valley of Rocks," dividing and forming an islet overgrown with wild rose and whortleberry. Above it stands Shilstone Tor, telling by its name that on it at one time stood a cromlech, which has been destroyed. This valley furnishes many studies for the artist.

Hence Yes Tor may be ascended, for long held to be the highest elevation on Dartmoor. The highest peak it is, rising to 2,030 feet, but it is overtopped by the rounded High Willhayes, 2,039 feet. Between Yes Tor and Mill Tor is a rather nasty bog. Mill Tor consists of a peculiar granite ; the feldspar is so pure that speculators have been induced to attempt to make soda-water bottles out of it, by fusing without the adjunct of other materials.

On the extreme edge of a ridge above the East Okement, opposite Belstone Tor, is a camp, much injured by the plough. Apparently from it leads a paved raised causeway or road, presumed to be Roman ; but why such a road should have been made from a precipitous headland above the Okement, and whither it led, are shrouded in mystery. Near this road, in 1897, was found a hoard of the smallest Roman coins, probably the store of some beggar, which he concealed under a rock, and died without being able to recover it. All pertained to the years between A.D. 320 and 330.

Of Okehampton I will say nothing here, as the place has had a chapter devoted to it in my *Book of*

the West—too much space, some might say, for in
itself it is devoid of interest.   Its charm is in the
scenery round, and its great attraction during the
summer is the artillery camp on the down above
Okehampton Park.   On the other side of Belstone,
Throwleigh may be visited, where there are numerous
prehistoric relics.   There were many others, but they
have been destroyed, amongst others a fine inclosure
like Grimspound, but more perfect, as the inclosing
wall was not ruinous throughout, and the stones were
laid in courses.   The pulpit of Throwleigh church is
made up of old bench-ends.

CHAPTER XI.

CHAGFORD

CHAGFORD is in Domesday written Chageford, and this is the local pronunciation of the name at the present day. The natives say, " Chageford in the dirt—O good Lord ! "

But Chagford has had the ability and promptitude to get out of the dirt and prove itself to be anything but a stick-in-the-mud place. It is with places as with people, some have good luck fall to them, others make their fortunes for themselves. Okehampton belongs to the former class, Chagford to the latter. It owes almost everything to a late rector, who, re-solved on pushing the place, invited down magazine editors and professional *littérateurs*, entertained them, drove them about, and was rewarded by articles appearing in journals and serials, belauding Chagford for its salubrious climate, its incomparable scenery, its ready hospitality, its rural sweetness, and its archæological interest.

Whither the writers pointed with their pens, thither the public ran, and Chagford was made. It has now every appliance suitable—pure water, electric lighting, telephone, a bicycle shop, and doctors to patch broken heads and set broken limbs of those upset from the "bikes."

Chagford is undoubtedly a picturesque and pleasant spot. It is situated near Dartmoor, and is sheltered from the cold and from the rainy drift that comes from the south-west. The lodging-house keepers know how to make visitors comfortable, and to charge for so doing. The church has been restored, coaches run to bring visitors, and the roads and lanes have been widened.

I recall the church before modern ideas had penetrated to Chagford. At that time the clerk, who also led the orchestra, gave out the psalm from his seat under the reading-desk, then, *whistling* the tune, he marched slowly down the nave, ascended to the gallery with leisure, and the performance began.

The church, dedicated to S. Michael, was rebuilt in the middle of the fifteenth century, when the Gorges family owned much land in the parish. Their cognisance, the *whirlpool*, a canting cognisance (*gurges*), appears in the bosses of the roof. It contains two monuments of some importance: one is a handsome stone altar tomb, with a canopy supported on columns, in memory of Sir John Whiddon, of Whiddon Park, Judge of Queen's Bench, who died in 1575; the other is to commemorate John Prouze, who died in 1664.

The Three Crowns Inn, opposite the church, is a

picturesque building of the seventeenth century. Chagford was one of the Stannary towns, but no remains of the court-house exist.

On Mattadon, above the town, stands a rude early cross of granite.

The ascent to the moor by Tincombe Lane, as I remember it half a century ago, was no better than a watercourse, strewn with boulders, to be scrambled up or down at the risk of dislocation of the ankle. It then well merited the descriptive lines :—

" Tincombe Lane is all uphill
    Or downhill, as you take it ;
  You tumble up, and crack your crown,
    Or tumble down and break it.

" Tincombe Lane is crook'd and straight,
    Here pothook, there as arrow,
  'Tis smooth to foot, 'tis full of rut,
    'Tis wide, and then, 'tis narrow.

" Tincombe Lane is just like life,
    From when you leave your mother ;
  'Tis sometimes this, 'tis sometimes that,
    'Tis one thing or the other."

Now all is changed. A steam-roller goes up and down Tincombe Lane, the angles have been rounded, the precipitous portions made easy, the ruts filled up. And life likewise is now made easy for the rising generation—possibly too easy. Ruggedness had a charm of its own, and bred vigour of constitution and moral physique.

Chagford having lost, by death, the whistling clerk, started a blind organist. Now, also, he is gone.

Every peculiarity is being crushed out of modern life by the steam-roller, civilisation.

Chagford Common, as I recall it, half a century ago, was strewn thick with hut circles. One ascended to it by Tincombe Lane and came into a prehistoric world, a Pompeii of a past before Rome was. It was dense with hut circles, pounds, and every sort of relic of the ancient inhabitants of the moor. But inclosures have been made, and but a very few relics of the aboriginal settlement remain. One of the most curious, the " Roundy Pound," only escaped through urgent remonstrance made to spare it. The road carried over the common annually eats up the remains of old, as the road-menders take away the stones from the hut circles to metal the highway.

At Batworthy, one of the inclosures, there must have been anciently a manufactory of flint tools and weapons. Countless spalls of flint and a fine collection of fabricated weapons and tools have been found there, and the collection has been presented from this place to the Plymouth Municipal Museum.

On Gidleigh Common, beside the Teign, opposite Batworthy, is Scaur Hill circle. It consists of thirty-two stones, at present, of which eight are prostrate. The highest of the stones is a little over six feet. The circle is ninety-two feet in diameter. Apparently leading towards this ring, on the Chagford side of the river, was a very long double row of stones, with a second double row or avenue branching from it.

There was a third double row, which started from the Longstone, near Caistor Rock. This Longstone is still standing, but the stone rows have been shame-

M

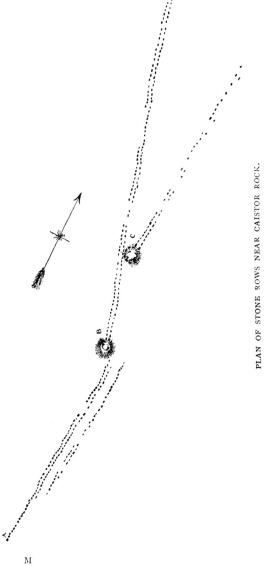

PLAN OF STONE ROWS NEAR CAISTOR ROCK.

(Taken in 1851. Scale 7½ in. to 10 feet.)

A. The Longstone. Hence in a northerly direction the row continued for 520 feet.

B. Cairn. C. Cairn with ring of stones.

fully robbed by a farmer to build his newtake walls. I give plan of the rows as taken by me in 1851. There was another line of stones leading from the Three Boys to the Longstone. The Three Boys were three big stones that have disappeared, and the line from them has also been obliterated. This portion I unfortunately did not plan in 1851.

In the valley of the Teign is the so-called tolmen, a natural formation. In the same slab or stone may be seen the beginnings of a second hole. But it is curious as showing that the river at one time rolled at a higher elevation than at present. The scenes on a ramble up the river from Chagford to Holy Street Mill and the mill itself are familiar to many, as having furnished subjects for pictures in the Royal Academy.

The river Teign below Whiddon Park winds in and out among wooded precipitous hills to where the Exeter road descends in zigzags to Fingle Bridge, passing on its way Cranbrook Castle, a stone camp. The *brook* in the name is a corruption of *burgh* or *burrh*. On the opposite side of the valley, frowning across at Cranbrook, is Prestonbury Camp.

With advantage the river may be followed down for several miles to Dunsford Bridge, and the opportunity is then obtained of gathering white heath which grows on the slopes. At Shilstone in Drewsteignton is the only cromlech in the county. It is a fine monument. A few years ago it fell, but has been re-erected in its old position. After recent ploughing flints may be picked up in the field where it stands.

Gidleigh merits a visit, the road to it presenting

many delicious peeps. Gidleigh possesses the ruin
of a doll castle that once belonged to the Prouze
family. The church contains a screen in good preservation. In the parish of Throwleigh is the
interesting manor house Wanson, of which I have
told a story in my *Old English Home.*

But perhaps more interesting than manor houses
are the old farm buildings in the neighbourhood of
Chagford, rapidly disappearing or being altered out
of recognition to adapt them to serve as lodging-
houses to receive visitors.

One such adaptation may be noticed in Tincombe
Lane. An old house is passed, where the ancient
mullioned windows have been heightened and the
floors and ceilings raised, to the lasting injury of
the house itself, considered from a picturesque point
of view. A passable road leads up the South Teign
to Fernworthy, a substantial farm in a singularly
lone spot. But there was another farm even more
lonely at Assacombe, where a lateral stream descends
to the Teign, but it has been abandoned, and consists now of ruin only. Near it is a well-preserved
double stone row leading from a cairn and finishing
at a blocking-stone.

At Fernworthy itself is a circle of upright stones
and the remains of several stone rows sorely mutilated
for the construction of a newtake wall. In a tumulus
near these monuments was found an urn containing
ashes, with a flint knife, and another, very small, of
bronze or copper, and a large polished button of
horn. On Chagford Common, near Watern Hill, is
a double pair of rows leading from a cairn and a

small menhir, to blocking - stones. Although the
stones of which they are composed are small, the
rows are remarkably well preserved.

It will repay the visitor to continue his ascent of
the South Teign to the Grey Wethers, two circles
of stone, of which, however, many are fallen. Here
exploration, such as has been conducted at Fernworthy circle, shows that the floors are deep in
ashes, and this leads to the surmise that the circles
were the crematories of the dead who lie in the
cairns and tunnels in the neighbourhood.

Near the source of the North Teign is Teignhead
House, one of the most solitary spots in England.
A shepherd resides there, but it is not for many
winters that a woman can endure the isolation and
retain her reason.

And yet there remain the ruins of a house in
a still more lonely situation. The moorman points
it out as Browne's House.

Although, judging from the dilapidation and the
lichened condition of the stones, one could have supposed that this edifice was of great antiquity, yet it
is not so by any means. There are those still alive
who remember when the chimney fell; and who had
heard of both the building, the occupying, and the
destruction of Browne's House. Few indeed have
seen the ruin, for it is in so remote a spot that only
the shepherd, the rush-cutter, and the occasional
fisherman approach it.

On the Ordnance Survey, faint indications of inclosures are given on the spot, but no name is
attached. Yet every moorman, if asked what these

GRIMSPOUND, AND ENTRANCE

ruins are, will tell you that it is the wreck of Browne's House.

The story told me relative to this solitary spot was that Browne, an ungainly, morose man, had a pretty young wife, of whom he was jealous. He built this place in which to live with her away from the society of men, and the danger such proximity might bring to his connubial happiness.

Grimspound will be visited from Chagford. The way to it after leaving the high-road from Post Bridge to Moreton, which it crosses, traverses Shapleigh Common, where are numerous inclosures in connection with hut circles. One of these is very large, and constructed of huge slabs of granite. Several of these larger circles were occupied only in summer, it would appear, as there are scanty traces of fire in them, whereas attached to them are small huts, the floors of which are thickly strewn with charcoal and fragments of pottery, and presumably the cooking was done in these latter.

Grimspound is an irregular circular inclosure containing four acres within the boundary wall. It is situated on the slope of a hill, and the position is obviously ill-adapted for defence, as it is commanded by higher ground on three sides. A little stream, the Grimslake, flows through the inclosure.

The wall itself is double-faced, and the two faces have fallen inwards. This shows that the core could not have been of turf, as in that case shrubs would have rooted themselves therein and have thrust the walls outward. In several places openings appear from the inside of the pound into the space between

the walls.   It is possible that this intermediate
hollow was used for stores, and that the walls were
tied together with timber, and surmounted with
a parapet of turf.   A trackway from Manaton to
Headland Warren runs through the pound, and the
wall has been broken through for this purpose in two
places; but the original entrance to the S.S.E. is
perfect, and is paved, and in it three steps have been
formed, as the descent was into the pound, another
token that the inclosure was not intended as a
fortress.

The entrance is 8 feet wide, and no outwork was
constructed to protect it from being "rushed" by an
enemy.   The walls of the inclosure here and
throughout are from 10 feet to 12 feet thick, and
stone does not exist in any part which could raise
them above 5 feet 6 inches in height.   Each wall
is 3 feet 6 inches wide at base, and was 3 feet at top.
On the west side is a huge slab set on edge, measuring 10 feet by 5 feet, and it is from 9 inches to 1 foot
in thickness, and weighs from 3 to 4 tons.   Other
stones, laid in courses, if not so long, are not of less
weight.   Such a wall as that inclosing Grimspound
would cost, with modern appliances and with horse
power for drawing the stone, three guineas per land
yard, and a land yard would engage four men for a
week.

When, moreover, we consider that the circumference of the wall measures over 1,500 feet, it becomes
obvious that a large body of men must have been
engaged in the erection.

Presumably Grimspound was not a fortified village,

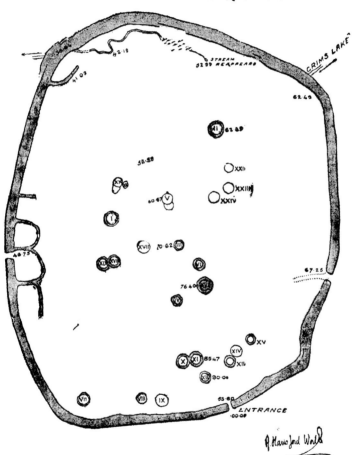

GRIMSPOUND

and was merely a pound into which cattle were driven for protection against wolves. It is just possible, but hardly probable, that it was the place of refuge for the scattered population on Hookner and Hamildon.

Within the pound are twenty-four hut circles; most have been explored, and one (No. III. on the plan) has been partially restored, and is inclosed within a railing. The object of this restoration was to discover, by piling up the stones found in and about the wall of the hut, what its height had been originally, and this was determined to have been four feet.

Unless wantonly injured by trippers, it will serve to exhibit what the structure of these habitations was, with its paved platform as bed, and its hearth and vestibule.

A double hut (XVIII., XIX.) is interesting because a tall stone was erected beside it, as though to indicate it as being the residence of some man of importance, maybe the sheik of the community. In hut XVI. is a double bed, one couch divided from the other by upright stones.

In several of the huts, in the floor, are laid flat stones with a smooth surface, and it was supposed that these served as chopping-stones, but further explorations have led to the belief that they were employed to sustain a central pole that upheld the roof.

On the *col* above Grimspound, near the source of Grimslake, is a cairn that contains a small kistvaen, and is surrounded by a circle of stones set upright.

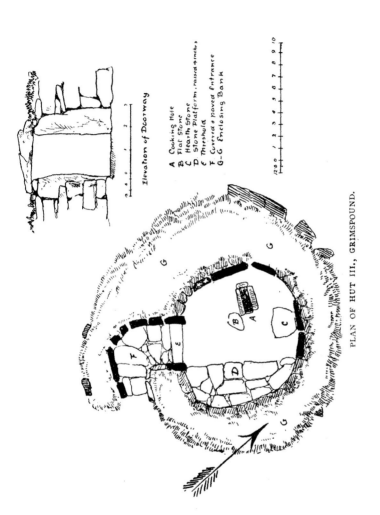

Elevation of Doorway

0 ½ 1 2 feet

A Cooking Hole
B Flat Stone
C Hearth Stone
D Stone Platform, raised 9 inches
E Threshold
F Curved & paved Entrance
G-G Enclosing Bank

1200 1 2 3 4 5 6 7 8 9 10 feet

PLAN OF HUT III., GRIMSPOUND.

Numerous cairns crown the heights. One immense tumulus, King's Barrow, has at some unknown time been excavated with great labour.

The great central trackway crosses Hamildon, and is very perfect where it does so. It had apparently no connection whatever with Grimspound.

From Grimspound may be seen, on the brow of the ridge connecting Birch Tor and Challacombe Down, a series of stone rows. They lead to a blocking-stone, or menhir, at the south extremity. The northern end has been destroyed by tin-streamers, whose works in Chaw Gully are interesting, for mining has been combined with streaming. The rock has been cut through, but no signs of the use of iron wedges for splitting the granite can here be discovered. It is traditionally told that what was done was to cut a groove in the granite, fill that with quicklime, and pour water on it. The lime in swelling split the rock. Ravens nest here; and I have seen rock doves and the pair of ravens nesting almost side by side.

Below is the Webburn, the stream turned up by tinners. There one mine continues in activity—the "Golden Dagger." Above is Vitifer, where fortunes have been made—and lost; mostly the latter by investors, mainly the former by the "captains" and promoters.

NEAR MANATON

CHAPTER XII.

MANATON

THE position of Manaton is one of remarkable
beauty, between Lustleigh Cleave and the ridge
on which stands Bowerman's Nose, and which swells
up to Hound Tor.

The church is dedicated to S. Winefred, the Welsh
martyr maid, and has its fine screen carefully restored.
It formerly possessed a singular feature, which the
"restoring" architect destroyed, because singular.
This was a small window in the east wall opening
from the outside, *under* the altar. Perhaps there
were relics of S. Winefred kept beneath the altar,
and through this *fenestrella confessionis* the devotees
could touch them. But, indeed, the destroyer has
been at Manaton and effaced more than this window.
On the tor that commands the village were formerly
many prehistoric monuments. The farm Langstone
by its name proclaims that on it was a menhir. In

the churchyard was a fine granite cross. A former
rector, the Rev. C. Carwithen, wantonly destroyed it
in the night. The people had been wont at a funeral
to carry the corpse the way of the sun thrice round
the cross before interment. He preached against the
custom ineffectually, so he secretly smashed the cross.
There are two logan rocks within easy reach—the
Whooping Stone on Easdon, and the Nutcracker in
Lustleigh Cleave.

This cleave is very picturesque. " Cleave " properly
is a local softening of the word " cliff," and applies to
the rocks, but in common use it has come incorrectly
to be applied to the valley below the crags. Through
the stone-strewn trough of the vale the sparkling
Bovey finds its way with some difficulty, diving
under the boulders at Horsham Steps, and running
unseen for some considerable distance, only proclaim-
ing its presence by its murmurs and whispers.

That there was some fighting done across this
valley is probable, because there are camps on both
sides.

In honourable contrast with Mr. Carwithen stands
Mr. Jones, the curate of North Bovey, who fished the
old village cross out of the brook, where it had lain
since the iconoclastic period of the Civil Wars, and
re-erected it in 1829.

North Bovey church, pleasantly situated, possesses
a screen much mutilated, but capable of restoration.
Far superior to it in preservation is that of Lustleigh,
which is of the same character as that of Bridford,
perhaps post-Reformation, and contains a series of
figures in the lower compartments representing clergy

in their caps and surplices and "liripipets," and not saints. There is some old glass in the church, in one window a representation of S. Margaret. There are monumental effigies in the church of the Prouze family. One of these is of Sir William Prouze, to whom the manor of Lustleigh belonged. By his will he directed that he should be buried with his ancestors at Lustleigh; but he died at a distance, and was interred at Holbeton. Some time after, the wishes of her father having come to the knowledge of Lady Alice, the wife of Sir Roger Mules, Baron of Cadbury, and finding that they had been disregarded, the dutiful daughter petitioned Grandisson, Bishop of Exeter in 1329, that the remains might be removed from Holbeton to Lustleigh, and the prayer was granted.

Forming the sill of the south door is a long granite stone with a Romano-British inscription, the reading of which has not been satisfactorily made out.

In the chancel may be noticed the stone brackets, perforated for the cords employed for the suspension of the Lenten veil.

A story associated with Lustleigh church has its parallels elsewhere. After it had been built the devil threatened to destroy it, stained glass and all, unless he were given a sacrifice. Now it happened that a bumpkin was present in the churchyard with a pack of cards in his pocket, and the Evil One immediately demanded him as his due; but the man, with great presence of mind, pounced on a cat that was stalking by and dashed out its brains against the wall of the porch. This satisfied the powers of darkness, and the consecration of the church followed. The story is a clumsy late cooking up of the old belief that before a building could be occupied a life must be sacrificed to the telluric deities. A horse, a dog, a sow—in this case a cat was offered up. Echoes of the same are found everywhere.* Most Devonshire churchyards were formerly supposed to be haunted by some animal or other, which had been buried under the corner-stone. When S. Columba took possession of Iona the question arose as to who was to die and be buried so as to secure the place for ever to the community. One of his monks, Oran by name, offered himself, and he was buried alive under the foundations of the new abbey.

The rectory house possesses its ancient hall open to the roof. In the hedge between the church and station is the "Bishop's Stone," a large block, bearing the arms of Bishop Stapeldon (1307-26), who was murdered in the riots occasioned by Edward II. favouring the Despensers. He was fallen on by the London mob in Cheapside, stripped, and beheaded by them.

Strewn about Lustleigh are numerous masses of granite, rounded, and like loaves of bread. This is due to the weathering of the granite, which is soft, but some, if not most, appear to have been carried to where they lie by water.

The stream Becka forms a fall into the valley of the Bovey, through woods, but except in very rainy

* See my article on "Foundations" in *Strange Survivals* (Methuen and Co., 1892). See also my *Book of the West*, i. p. 331.

HOUND TOR

weather it is insignificant, and hardly merits to be considered a waterfall; it is properly only a water-trickle.

The eastern flank of the moor is infinitely richer in vegetation than the western. The whole of Dartmoor stands up as a wall against the prevalent north-west and south-west winds that distort the trees on the west side. Moreover, owing to the shelter thus furnished, and to the disintegration of the granite trending in this direction so as to form deep beds of gravel, the valleys and hillsides are clothed with rich vegetation. Pines flourish.

Hound Tor is a noble mass of rocks. It derives its name from the shape assumed by the blocks on the summit, that have been weathered into forms resembling the heads of dogs peering over the natural battlements, and listening to hear the merry call of the horn. Below it, on the Manaton side, nestles Hound Tor Farm, picturesquely enfolded in a sycamore grove.

The sycamore, by the way, is peculiarly the tree for Dartmoor and other exposed situations. The beech cowers and turns from the blast, and it divides so soon as its taproot touches rock; but the sycamore stands up, indifferent to wind and rain, to which it opposes the broad green leaves that it turns against the blast, and so shelters itself as with scale armour.

On Hound Tor is a circle of stones containing a kistvaen.

The road that leads to Widdecombe and Ashburton ascends to Hound Tor; but there is another road to Ashburton by Hey Tor that branches off to the left before Hound Tor Farm is reached, and scrambles up to Trendlebere Down, passing an almost destroyed stone row starting from a cairn beside the highway. The road runs at a great elevation (1,080 feet) for some miles. There is a pleasant and homely inn at Hey Tor Vale, where the traveller may rest and gather strength to visit Holwell Tor and Hey Tor Rocks. Holwell Tor was at one time surrounded by a stone rampart, but quarrymen have sadly injured it, and it is not now easy to decide whether the inclosure was merely a pound, like Grimspound, or a stone camp, like Whit Tor.

Hey Tor Rocks form two fine masses, and are unlike most of the moorland tors, in that the granite is very consistent, and is not broken into the usual layers of soft beds alternating with hard layers. The view of the valley below Hey Tor and Grea Tor on one side, and the ridge of Bone Hill on the other, is fine.

The road, commanding to the east a vast stretch of the rich lowlands of Devon, passes Saddle Tor and reaches Rippon Tor, where is a good logan stone. Here are several cairns much mutilated by the road-makers. On the further side of the road, by Pill Tor, are remains of an extensive prehistoric settlement. Many huts and inclosures remain. The place bears the name of Foale's Arrishes, from a man of that appellation who spent his energies in converting the prehistoric inclosures into fields for his own use, to the destruction of much that was

HEY TOR

interesting, and to his own very dubitable advantage. The huts have, however, yielded fine specimens of ornamented pottery. The decoration is here and there made with a woman's finger-nail. Consider that! Some poor barbaric squaw five thousand years ago fashioned the damp clay with her hands and devised a rude pattern, which she incised with her

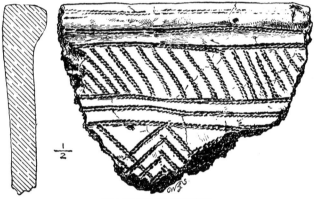

FRAGMENT OF POTTERY.

nails. She is long ago gone to dust, and her dust dispersed, but the impress of her nails remains.

This is much like what we are all doing, and doing unconsciously—leaving little finger-touches on our creations, giving shape to the minds and habits of our children and of those with whom we are brought into contact, shaping, adorning, or disfiguring our epoch, and the impressions we leave are indelible; they will in turn be transmitted to ages to come.

Some of the ornamentation, as in a specimen from

N

Smallacombe Rocks, is made with a twisted cord. The pottery is all hand-made, shaped without the wheel, and very imperfectly burnt. It is not red, because there was little iron in the clay.

One large hut at Foale's Arrishes had a seat carried round part at least of the interior, made of branches that were held from spreading by sharp stones planted upright in the floor. The kitchen was on the left side of the entrance in a subsidiary structure.

It has, of late, become a thing not unusual for young fellows, if suffering from delicacy of the lungs, to rent or buy a farm on Dartmoor. No research after parasitic microbes thenceforth concerns them. The fresh air, the constant exercise, the joyous existence on the wild moor are fatal to tubercular bacteria. Rude health, buoyant spirits, unflagging energy result from such treatment.

It is, it must be admitted, surpassing hard to induce servants from the "in-country" to take situations on Dartmoor. The air there is as unsuited to them as to other microbes. But the settler lights his own fires, cooks his own meals, makes his own bed; and, as one of them assured me, his experience proved to him that a man can keep a hunter at the same cost as he can a servant-maid: therefore, why be worried with the latter?

At Post Bridge they have had a succession of curates who have lived this life in cabins or hovels, and have learned to love it. It has one drawback, and one only—it makes the hands rough and grimy. But what are gloves for, but to cover dirty hands when we go to town to make display?

As to food. Rabbits are to be had at any moment; geese, ducks live and luxuriate on the moor; an occasional blackcock or moorhen and a brace of snipe give zest; and trout are to be obtained for the labour or pleasure of angling for them. The price of horses is mounting; any number may be grown on the moor. Sheep, cattle—you turn them

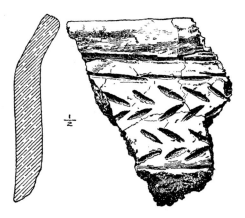

ORNAMENTED POTTERY.

out, and they thrive on the sweet grass, and know not the maladies that afflict flocks and herds in the world twelve hundred feet below.

Let it not be supposed that in winter Dartmoor is a desolation and a horror. It is by no means an unpleasant place for a sojourn then. When below are mud and mist, aloft on the moor the ground is hard with frost and the air crisp and clear. Down below we are oppressed with the fall of the leaf,

affecting us, if inclined to asthma and bronchitis;
and in the short, dull days of December and January
our spirits wax dark amidst naked trees and when
our ankles are deep in mud. There are no trees on
Dartmoor to expose their naked limbs, and tell us
that vegetation is dead. The shoulders of down are
draped in brown sealskin mantles—the ling and
heather, as lovely in its sleep as in its waking state;
the mosses, touched by frost, turn to rainbow hues.
For colour effects give me Dartmoor in winter.

And then the peat fires! What fires can surpass
them? They do not flame, but they glow, and
diffuse an aroma that fills the lungs with balm.
The turf-cutting is one of the annual labours on
the moor. Every farm has its peat-bog, and in the
proper season a sufficiency of fuel·is cut, then carried
and stacked for winter use. I may be mistaken, but
it seems to me that cooking done over a peat fire
surpasses cooking at the best club in London. But
it may be that on the moor one relishes a meal in a
manner impossible elsewhere.

Widdecombe-in-the-Moor is a village in a valley
walled off from the world by high ridges on the east
and on the west. The entire bed of the valley has
been washed and rewashed by streamers for tin.
Bag Park is a gentleman's seat laid out on this collection of refuse, and the pines and firs luxuriate in
the granite rubble and grow, as if it were to them
a pleasure to thrust up their leaders and expand their
boughs.

I shall never forget a drive through Widdecombe
one October day, when the sun was shining bright,

and the air was soft. The sycamores had shed their leaves; but the expedition was one through coral land. The rowan or mountain-ash, which was everywhere, was burdened with clusters of scarlet berries, and the hedges were wreathed with rose-hips and dense with ruddy haws.

The church of Widdecombe has a very fine tower, built, it is said, by the tinners. The roof has many of the original bosses, carved and painted with heads, flowers, and leaves. One has the figure on it of S. Catherine with her wheel. One boss has on it three rabbits, each with a single ear, which unite in the centre, forming a triangle. One exactly similar is in Tavistock church.

Part of the lower portion of the roodscreen remains with figures of saints on it.

The story of the great thunderstorm in which Widdecombe church was struck, on Sunday, October 21st, 1638, when the congregation were present at divine service, has often been told, notably by Mr. Blackmore in his novel *Christowel*.

Prince, in his *Worthies of Devon*, thus narrates the circumstances :—

"In the afternoon, in service time, there happened a very great darkness, which still increased to that degree, that they could not see to read; soon after, a terrible and fearful thunder was heard, like the noise of so many great guns, accompanied with dreadful lightning, to the great amazement of the people; the darkness still increasing, that they could not see each other, when there presently came such an extraordinary flame of lightning, as filled the church with fire, smoak, and a loathsome smell, like brim-

stone; a ball of fire came in likewise at the window, and
passed through the church, which so affrighted the congregation, that most of them fell down in their seats; some
upon their knees, others on their faces, and some one upon
another, crying out of burning and scalding, and all giving
themselves up for dead.   There were in all four persons
killed, and sixty-two hurt, divers of them having their linen
burnt, tho' their outward garments were not so much as
singed. . . . The church itself was much torn and defaced
with the thunder and lightning, a beam whereof, breaking
in the midst, fell down between the minister and clerk, and
hurt neither.   The steeple was much wrent; and it was
observed where the church was most torn, there the least
hurt was done among the people.   There was none hurted
with the timber or stone; but one man, who, it was judged,
was killed by the fall of a stone."

The monument of this man, Roger Hill, is in
the church, as also an account in verse of the storm,
composed by the village schoolmaster.

For many years the incumbent of Widdecombe
was a man who was reputed to be the son of
George IV. when Prince Regent.   His sister, married
to a captain, who deserted her, occupied a cottage,
now in ruins, under Crockern Tor.   She also was
believed to be of blood-royal with a bar sinister.
Both the parson and his sister had been brought
up about Court.   He, when given the living of
Widdecombe—to get him out of sight and mind—
brought with him a large consignment of excellent
port, and that drew to his parsonage such rare men
as would brave the moors and storms for the sake
of a carouse.

His sister, in the desolate cottage under Crockern Tor, languished and died, leaving her only child, Caroline, to the charge of her uncle. She was sent for her education to a famous school in Queen's Square, London, where she associated with girls belonging to families of the first rank.

A certain air of distinction, as well as the story that circulated relative to her mother's origin, made her an object of interest, and her imperious manner commanded respect.

The vicarage was by no means a good place in which a young girl should grow to maturity. The house was not frequented by men of the best character, and the wildest stories are told of the goings-on there in the forties and fifties.

Caroline was, however, a girl of exceptionally strong character; she was early called on to hold her own with the associates of her uncle and frequenters of the vicarage, and she was quite able to enforce upon them a proper behaviour towards herself.

Unhappily, she had been reared without any religious principles; her law was consequently her own caprice, fortunately held in check by a strong sense of personal dignity.

The position she was in was as forlorn and unpromising as any in which a young girl could find herself.

She was full of generous impulses, but they were wholly untrained; she possessed furious passions, which were held in check solely by her pride. She would do at one time a generous act and next a dirty trick, "just," as the people said, "as though she were a pixy."

A gentleman named Darke, visiting her uncle on some business, married Caroline, and soon after her uncle died suddenly, having made a will in her favour.

The vicarage was well furnished and contained articles of great value, in pictures, plate, etc., supposed to have been presented to him, but most likely obtained with money lent at Court to those temporarily embarrassed.

The manor had been sold, and was purchased by Mrs. Darke's trustees at her request, and from that time she insisted on being entitled "Lady" Darke; and into this she moved with her dogs, horses, and husband.

This latter had soon discovered what an imperious character she possessed. His will might clash with hers, but hers would never give way. Her character was the toughest and most energetic, and by degrees he fell into a condition of submission and insignificance which it was painful to witness, and which "Lady" Darke herself resented, without being aware that it was due to her own overbearing behaviour.

She kept nine or ten horses in her stables—some had never been broken in; some she rode on, others were driven in pairs. But towards the end of her life the horses were not taken out, and ate their heads off many times over.

If a visitor of distinction was expected, she sent for him her carriage and pair with silver-mounted harness. For ordinary use she employed her brass-mounted harness; but Bill, her husband, was despatched to market in the little trap in which she fetched coals. Latterly Mr. Darke was sent to make purchases at Ashburton, with a long list of "chores," *i.e.* of articles he was to bring back with him, written out during the week on a slip of paper from a pocket-book. Here is one: "Kidney-beans and cucumbers; tea, and green paint with driers; brushes and putty; sweets; and a frock-body for myself; a milkpan, fourteen inches; side-combs, 3*s.* 6*d.*; ostler's boy and fish; lavender; pain-killer; wine, salad oil, harness paste, and rice; also ribs of beef, grate for blue bedroom, india-rubber; rabbits, grind scissors, cheese, inn and ostler."

She ruled her husband, and indeed everyone with whom she came in contact. He, cut off from social intercourse with his fellows, out of the current of intellectual life, with no other work to do than to fulfil her behests, sank in his own estimation, and fell into degradation without making an effort to rise out of it.

An instance of her despotic character may be given. One day she wanted to have her hay made; she was anxious lest a change of weather should come on. She issued an imperious order to the curate of the parish to come and help save the hay. He sent an apology. This rendered her furious. She went in quest of him, met him in the village, and falling on him soundly boxed his ears in public.

She was an implacable hater; and living on the wilds, half educated, she was superstitious, and believed in witchcraft, and in her own power to ill-

wish such individuals as offended her. She was
caught on one occasion with a doll into which she
was sticking pins and needles, in the hope and with
the intent thereby of producing aches and cramps in
a neighbour. On another occasion she laid a train of
gunpowder on her hearth, about a figure of dough,
and ignited it, for the purpose of conveying an
attack of fever to the person against whom she was
animated with resentment.

It need hardly be said that believing in her own
powers others believed in them as well, and dreaded
offending her.

She was kind-hearted, and impulsive in her
generosity. She divided the parish into two halves
—one she gave over to the doctor and kept the other
to herself. " He kills with his physic," she said, " I
keep alive and recover with my soups and port wine."

She was vastly angry with the vicar, her uncle's
successor, about some trifle, and she went after him
with her whip and threatened to chastise him with
it. He actually summoned her, and swore that he
lived in bodily fear of the lady.

She liked to have visitors drop in on her, but not
to be warned of their coming ; for she took a pride
in showing what she could provide for table on the
spur of the moment ; and forth would come a ham,
half a goose, a boiled leg of mutton, a big cheese
and celery, produced as by magic, and would be
served by herself in an old gown, red turnover hand-
kerchief on her shoulders, and a coalscuttle bonnet
on her head.

Mrs. Darke at one time played on the piano after

the meal to get her guests to dance, but the cats tore
the instrument open and made their nests and kittened
among the strings, and the damp air rusted the wires.
Then she bought a barrel-organ, and forced her
husband to turn the handle in the corner and grind
out the music for the dancers. However, on one
occasion, having tasted too often a bottle within
reach, though out of sight, he fell forward in the
middle of a dance and brought the instrument down
with him. The instrument was so broken that it
could no longer be used. Mr. Darke died at last in
one of the fits to which he was liable, having retired
to rest by mistake under in place of on the bed.

By this time the lady had become very deaf.

On hearing the news of the decease some friends
went to see her.

"Very grieved, madam, at your sad loss!"

"Ah! Bill is dead. He might have done worse;
he might have lived. You will stop and dine, of
course."

They had to tarry to see to matters of business.
"Now, look here," said "Lady" Darke, "I'll have no
more 'truck' with Bill. He has been trouble to me
long enough. I shall send him to his friends in
Plymouth. Let them bury him."

"Madam," said the nurse, "we want to lay him
out. Will you give me a sheet?"

"A sheet! One of my good linen sheets! Not I.
Take a pig-cloth"; that is to say, one in which bacon
was salted. And actually her husband was laid in
his coffin in one of these "pig-cloths."

In Mrs. Cudlip's novel, *She Cometh Not, He Saith*,

is a description of a meeting with the lady that is
very true to life, as is also the account of the downstairs arrangement of the manor house.

In later years "Lady" Darke became infirm. She
neglected everything, and no one dared do anything
in the house without her orders. Until she came
downstairs in the morning there could be no break-
fast, as she kept the keys. The house was infested
with cats and dogs, and her servants did not dare
to get rid of any of them, or to drive them out of the
rooms. The large room over the kitchen she alone
entered. The door was padlocked, and the key of
the padlock she kept attached to her garter. Thence
the key had to be taken after her death to obtain
admission. It was found to contain a confused mass
of sundry articles to the depth of three feet above the
floor, the accumulation of many years. Bureaus were
there with guineas and banknotes in the drawers,
and quantities of old silver plate, bearing the arms
and crests of men of title who had been about the
Court of the Prince Regent; and the whole was
veiled in cobwebs that hung from the ceiling so long
and so dense as to hide the further extremity of the
chamber.

"Lady" Darke retained her imperious disposition
to the end; it was in vain that it was suggested to
her that she should have an attendant to be always
with her. She often sat up the whole night by her
fire, and her servants dared not retire to bed till their
mistress had given the signal that they were to
depart.

Of relations she had none; at least none who

came near her, and when she was dead much
difficulty was found in discovering any persons who
had claim to her inheritance.

She died quite suddenly, and left no will.

Her trustees had to advertise before they could
find relations, and then those who presented themselves were the children of her father by a third
wife. Her dogs and cats were first killed, then
several old horses that were dragging themselves
about the field in extreme old age.

Her plate and pictures were sold.

To the best of my knowledge no portrait of her
remains.

She was a fine woman, and must at one time have
been handsome. It was fancied by many that her
features bore a resemblance to the pictures of
George IV. in his young days. The mystery
relative to her mother and uncle was never solved,
and it is possible enough that the supposed paternity
was due to idle gossip.

There were vast collections of letters among the
remains, but these were all destroyed, and nothing
was allowed to transpire as to their contents.

The story from beginning to end is one of infinite
sadness. It is of one with a remarkably strong but
undisciplined character, one full of good impulses,
who had never been taught religious duty, and given
no religious belief, who was therefore condemned to
waste a profitless life in a remote village, without
purpose, without self-discipline, without hope, without
God.

There are some interesting old farmhouses about

Widdecombe ; one is at Chittleford, another on Corndon. The primitive type of farm on the moor was an inclosed courtyard, entered through a gate. Opposite the gate is the dwelling-house, with a projecting porch, with an arched granite door and a mullioned window over it. On one side of the entrance is the dwelling-room, on the other the saddle and sundry chamber. The well, which is a stream of water from the moor conducted by a small leat to the house, is under cover ; and the cattle-sheds open into the yard, so as to be reached with ease from the house without exposure to the storms.

These farm dwellings are rapidly disappearing, and are making way for more pretentious and extremely hideous buildings. Such as remain are remarkably picturesque, and should be photographed before they are destroyed.

Widdecombe must not be quitted without a reference to the famous ballad of the old grey mare taken there to the fair ; a ballad that is immensely popular in Devon, and one to the air of which the Devon Regiment went against the Boers.

"Tom Pearce, Tom Pearce, lend me thy grey mare,
    All along, down along, out along, lee.
  For I want for to go to Widdecombe Fair,
    Wi' Bill Brewer, Jan Stewer, Peter Gurney, Peter Davy,
    Dan'l Whiddon, Harry Hawk,
  Old Uncle Tom Cobleigh and all.
        Chorus—Old Uncle Tom Cobleigh and all.

"And when shall I see again my grey mare?
    All along, down along, out along, lee.
  By Friday soon, or Saturday noon,
    Wi' Bill Brewer, etc.

LOWER TARR

" Then Friday came, and Saturday noon,
    All along, down along, out along, lee.
But Tom Pearce's old mare hath not trotted home,
    Wi' Bill Brewer, etc.

" So Tom Pearce he got up to the top of the hill
    All along, down along, out along, lee.
And he seed his old mare down a-making her will,
    Wi' Bill Brewer, etc."

Now it does not appear from the song *why* the
mare was so dead beat.   But a clever American
artist, who has illustrated the song, has brought her
knowledge of human nature to bear on the story.
She has shown in her pictures how that the borrower

of the horse met with a pretty gipsy girl at the fair, and persuaded her to ride away with him *en croupe*. This explains at once why the horse was so overcome that it "fell sick and died."

One can understand also how that this ballad being a man's song, a veil is delicately thrown over this incident.

I do not quote the entire ballad.

> "When the wind whistles cold on the moor of a night,
>   All along, down along, out along, lee.
> Tom Pearce's old mare doth appear ghastly white,
>   Wi' Bill Brewer, etc.

> "And all the long night be heard skirling and groans,
>   All along, down along, out along, lee.
> From Tom Pearce's old mare in her rattling bones,
>   Wi' Bill Brewer, etc."

CHAPTER XIII.

HOLNE

Holne church and screen—Epitaph—Holne Chase—The Coffin-stone
—Dartmeet Bridge—Dolly's Cot—Dolly Trebble—Sherrill—Var
Tor—Proposed new road—Pixy Holt—Blowing-house at Okebrook
—Jolly Lane Cot—Song-hunting under difficulties—The Sandy
Way—Childe's Tomb—Crosses in a line—Swincombe—Gobbetts
Mine—Crazing-mill stones—Holne vicarage—Charles Kingsley—
Old customs at Holne—Similar custom at King's Teignton—
Sacrifice of sheep.

AT Holne the old church house, now an inn,
affords very comfortable quarters, and from it
many interesting excursions may be made.

Holne church has preserved its old screen and
pulpit, the former rich with paintings of saints. Both
were probably erected by Oldam, Bishop of Exeter,
1504-19. In the churchyard is the following doggerel
inscription :—

" Here lies poor old Ned, on his last mattrass bed.
　　During life he was honest and free ;
He knew well the chase, but has now run his race,
　　And his name it was Colling, d'ye see.
　　　He died December 28th, 1780, aged 77."

From the vicarage garden a noble view of the
windings of the Dart through Holne Chase is to
be obtained—permission asked and given.

To see Holne Chase, it should be ascended as far

as New Bridge, and thence descended through the Buckland Drives. Permission is given on fixed days.

In Holne Wood, where the river makes a loop, is an early camp, with indications of hut circles in it, but thrown out of shape by the trees growing in the area. Near the entrance charcoal-burners have formed their hole in which to burn the timber. A finer and better preserved camp is Hembury.

In the Chase, on the Buckland side under Awsewell Rock, are the remains of furnaces and great heaps of slag. The point is where there is a junction of the granite and the sedimentary rocks. Above the wooded flank of the hill, the rocks are pierced and honey-combed by miners following veins of ore, probably copper. The workings are very primitive, and deserve inspection. The little village of Buckland should not be neglected. It is marvellously pic-turesque, but the houses do not appear to be healthy, being buried in foliage. The church has not been restored. It possesses an old screen with curious paintings, some impossible to interpret; and it is in the old bepewed, neglected condition familiar now only to those whose years number something about sixty or seventy. Buckland-in-the-Moor is the full name of this parish, but it is no longer in the moor. Colonel Bastard, ancestor of the present owner, planted all the heathery land and hillsides with trees, and received therefor the thanks of Parliament as one who by so doing had deserved well of his country.

If Holne Chase be beautiful, so is the Dart above New Bridge. A more interesting drive can hardly be taken than one branching off from the main road before reaching Pound's Gate and following a grassy track called " Dr. Blackall's Drive," that sweeps round the heights above the Dart and rejoins the road between Mel Tor and Sharpie Tor.

But to see the Dart valley in perfection the river should be followed up on foot from New Bridge to that of Dartmeet, and thence up to Post Bridge.

The descent to Dartmeet by the road is one of over five hundred feet.   Halfway is the Coffin-stone, on which five crosses are cut, and which is split in half—the story goes, by lightning.   On this it is customary to rest a dead man on his way from the moor beyond Dartmeet to his final resting-place at Widdecombe.   When the coffin is laid on this stone, custom exacts the production of the whisky bottle, and a libation all round to the manes of the deceased.

One day a man of very evil life, a terror to his neighbours, was being carried to his burial, and his corpse was laid on the stone whilst the bearers regaled themselves.   All at once, out of a passing cloud shot a flash, and tore the coffin and the dead man to pieces, consuming them to cinders, and splitting the stone.   Do you doubt the tale?   See the stone cleft by the flash.

Among the many hundreds who annually visit Dartmeet, I do not suppose that more than one sees the real beauties to which this spot opens the way.   Actually, Dartmeet Bridge is situated at the least interesting and least picturesque point on the river.

To know the Dart and see its glories, a visitor

must desert the bridge and ascend the river. I will indicate to him two walks, each of remarkable beauty and each an easy one.

The first is this: Ascend the Dart on the *left*. This can be done by passing through a gate above Dartmeet Cottage, and descending to the river, where remain a few of the venerable oaks that once abounded at Brimpts, but were wantonly cut down at the beginning of this century. Ascend by a fisherman's path through the plantation to where the wood ends, and the hills falling back reveal a pleasant meadow, with, rising out of it by the river, a holt or pile of rocks overgrown with oaks. The view from this is beautiful. Proceeding half a mile a ruined cottage is reached, where the stately Yar Tor may be seen to advantage. This ruin is called Dolly's Cot.

Dolly, who has given her name to this ruin, was a somewhat remarkable woman. She lived with her brother, orphans, by Princetown when Sir Thomas Tyrwhitt settled at Tor Royal. She was a remarkably handsome girl, and she seems to have caught the eye of this gentleman, who located her and her brother in the lodge, and then, as the brother kept a sharp look-out on his sister, he got rid of him by obtaining for him an appointment in the House of Lords, where he looked after the lighting, and had as his perquisite the ends of the wax tapers. As fresh candles were provided every day, and the sessions were at times short, the perquisites were worth a good deal.

However, if the brother were away Dolly had

THE CLEFT ROCK ABOVE HOLNE CHASE

another to watch over her, one Tom Trebble, a young and handsome moorman, who did not at all relish the manner in which Sir Thomas, Warden of the Stannaries, hovered about Miss Dolly.

But a climax was reached when the Prince Regent arrived at Tor Royal to visit his forest of Dartmoor. The Prince's eye speedily singled Dolly out, and the blue coat and brass buttons, white ducks tightly strapped, and the curled-brimmed hat were to be seen on the way to Dolly's cottage a little too frequently to please Tom Trebble. So to cut his anxieties short he whisked Dolly on to the pillion of his moor cob and rode off with her to Lydford, where they were married. Then he carried her away to this cottage—now a ruin—on the Dart, to which led no road, hardly a path even, and where she was likely to be out of the way of both the Prince and his humble servant, Sir Thomas.

In this solitary cottage Tom and Dolly lived for many years. She survived her husband, and gained her livelihood by working at the tin-mine of Hexworthy, where one of the shafts recently sunk was named after her.

The candle-snuffer realised—so it was said—a good fortune out of the wax taper-ends, and never returned to Dartmoor.

Dolly lived to an advanced age, and even as an old woman was remarkably handsome and of a distinguished appearance.

It is now difficult to collect authentic information concerning her, as only very old people remember Dolly. She was buried at Widdecombe, and aged

moor folk still speak of her funeral, at which all
the women mourners wore white skirts, *i.e.* their
white petticoats *without* the coloured skirts of their
gowns, and white kerchiefs pinned as crossovers to
cover their shoulders.

The distance is between six and seven miles.
Dolly was borne to her grave by the tin-miners,
and followed not only by the mine-workers, but
by all the women of the moorside, and all in
their white petticoats; and as they went they
sang psalms.

From Dolly's Cot the hill can be ascended to
'The Seven Sisters," seven conspicuous old Scotch
pines, whereof one has lost its head. Thence a
road is reached that takes a visitor back to Dartmeet by Brimpts.

The other walk, even finer, is this: Ascend the
hill on the Ashburton road till a road breaks away
to the left to Sherrill. Follow this, when on the *col*
a kistvaen, inclosed in a circle, is reached. North of
this is a much-ruined set of stone rows, three parallel
lines running 660 feet, but so plundered that only
158 stones remain. The road descends to a pleasant
little settlement, Sherrill, or Sher-well, consisting of
a farm and some cottages. The Sher-well bursts
out in one strong spring beside the road, and becomes
a good stream almost directly.

The situation is warm and sheltered, and the
ground is cultivated. The road descends to the
Wallabrook, which it crosses, to Babeney. Thence
a track leads down the Wallabrook to its junction
with the Dart, where is disclosed what I hold to be one

YAR TOR

of the finest, if not the finest view on Dartmoor.
A tract of level pasture lies at the junction of
the streams, and from this Yar Tor soars up a
veritable mountain. Few of the Dartmoor heights
are so situated as to show themselves to such advantage. On the right, a spur well clothed in dark
fir plantations comes down from Brimpts; and on
the left is a clitter of bold granite rocks. The time
to visit this is certainly the evening, when Yar Tor is
bathed in a golden glory, and the woods are steeped
in royal purple.

Thence a path, or track rather, leads down the Dart
on the east side, past Badgers' Holt to the bridge.

And perhaps on the way the *Graphis scripta* may be
found, but it is chiefly to be discovered on old hollies,
a mysterious writing, characters scrawled by delicate
hands, and understandable only by the pixies, who
are credited with thus writing their messages to one
another. Actually this is a lichen, that strangely
affects a script.

It was at Badgers' Holt that old Dan Leaman
lived, on whom a trick was played which I have
already related in my *Book of the West*.

What a solitary life must have been led by the
occupants of the scattered farms and cottages at
Babeney, Sherrill, Dury, and the like, in former times!
And yet those who occupied them got to love the
isolation. A woman at Sherrill, who had been in
service and had married a moorman, said to me, " I
wouldn't live here if I could help it ; but, Lor' bless y',
my old man, there's no gettin' he away from atop o'
Widdecombe chimney"—that is to say, the level of the

church tower. The reach of its bells formed the world—the only world in which he cared to live. In a cottage near Sherrill lived an old woman absolutely alone, who for sixty years never once allowed her fire to go out.

If it be desired to open out Dartmoor, a road should be carried up the Dart from New Bridge to Dartmeet, and thence, still following the river, to Post Bridge. The owners of the banks of the Dart below New Bridge to Holne Bridge—in fact, of Holne Chase—could then hardly refuse to allow it to be carried through their land to Holne Bridge, and then a drive would be created passing through scenery unsurpassed in England. Another ought to be engineered up the Webburn from its meet with the Dart, past Lizwell to Widdecombe ; then that solitary village would be at once accessible, and brought into the world.

Below Dartmeet Bridge, if the river be followed on the right through a wood, the Pixy Holt is reached, a cave in which the little good folk are supposed to dwell. It is the correct thing to leave a pin or some other trifle in acknowledgment when visiting their habitation.

Where the Okebrook drops into the West Dart is an old blowing-house, with moulds for the tin, ruined, and with a stout oak growing up in the midst. There are also mortar-stones in the ruin. Above Huccaby Bridge are the remains of a fine circle of standing stones that has been sadly muti- lated. Another, far more perfect, is at Sherberton.

Near the bridge is Jolly Lane Cot, the house of

Sally Satterleigh, that was built and occupied in one day. Her father was desirous of marrying a wife and bringing her to a home; but he had no home to which to introduce her, and the farmers round not only would afford no help, but proved obstructive. One day when it was Holne Revel, and the farmers had gone thither, the labouring people assembled in swarms, set to work and built up the cottage, and before the farmers returned, lively with drink, from the revel, the man was in the cottage and had lighted a fire on the hearth, and this constituted a freeholding from which no man might dispossess him. This man was a notable singer, and his old daughter, now a grandmother, remembered some of his songs. One wild and stormy day, Mr. Bussell, of Brazen Nose College, now Dr. Bussell and tutor of his college, drove over with me from Princetown to get her songs from her.

But old Sally could not sit down and sing. We found that the sole way in which we could extract the ballads from her was by following her about as she did her usual work. Accordingly we went after her when she fed the pigs, or got sticks from the firewood rick, or filled a pail from the spring, pencil and notebook in hand, dotting down words and melody. Finally she did sit to peel some potatoes, when Mr. Bussell with a MS. music-book in hand, seated himself on the copper. This position he maintained as she sang the ballad of " Lord Thomas and the Fair Eleanor," till her daughter applied fire under the cauldron, and Mr. Bussell was forced to skip from his perch.

Holne forms the extreme eastern end of a long ridge that terminates to the west in Down Tor. This hog's back stands over 1,500 feet above the sea, and is the watershed. From it stream the Avon, the Erme, the Yealm, and the Plym in a southerly direction, and north of it are the West Dart and the Swincombe river. It is a rounded back of moor, without granite tors, thickly sown with bogs. But there is a track, the Sandy Way, that threads these morasses from Holne, and leads to Childe's Tomb, a kistvaen, with a cross near it.

The story is well known.

A certain Childe, a hunter, lost his way in winter in this wilderness. Snow fell thick and his horse could go no further.

> " In darkness blind, he could not find
>   Where he escape might gain,
>   Long time he tried, no track espied,
>   His labours all in vain.
>
> " His knife he drew, his horse he slew
>   As on the ground it lay ;
>   He cut full deep, therein to creep,
>   And tarry till the day.
>
> " The winds did blow, fast fell the snow,
>   And darker grew the night,
>   Then well he wot he hope might not
>   Again to see the light.
>
> " So with his finger dipp'd in blood,
>   He scrabbled on the stones—
>   ' This is my will, God it fulfil,
>   And buried be my bones.
>
> " ' Whoe'er it be that findeth me,
>   And brings me to a grave ;
>   The lands that now to me belong
>   In Plymstock he shall have.' "

The story goes on to say that when the monks of Buckfast heard of this they made ready to transport the body to their monastery. But the monks of Tavistock were beforehand with them; they threw a bridge over the Tavy, ever after called Guile Bridge, and carried the dead Childe to their abbey. Thenceforth they possessed the Plymstock estate.

The kistvaen is, of course, not Childe's grave, for it is prehistoric, and Childe was not buried there. But the cross may have been set up to mark the spot where he was found.

Childe's Cross was quite perfect, standing on a three-stepped pedestal, till in or about 1812, when it was nearly destroyed by the workmen of a Mr. Windeatt, who was building a farmhouse near by. The stones that composed it have, however, been for the most part recovered, and the cross has been restored as well as might be under the circumstances.

The Sandy Way was doubtless a very ancient track across the moor from east to west, as it is marked by crosses, as may be judged by the Ordnance map. 1, Horne's Cross; 2 and 3, crosses on Down Ridge; 4 and 5, crosses on Terhill; 6 and 7, crosses near Fox Tor, in the Newtake; 8, Childe's Cross; 9, Seward's or Nun's Cross; 10, cross on Walkhampton Common.

Swincombe, formerly Swan-combe, runs to the north of the ridge, and has the sources of its river in the Fox Tor mires and near Childe's Tomb.

It runs north-east, and then abruptly passes north to decant into the West Dart.

Near this is Gobbetts Mine, a very interesting

spot, for here are samples of the modern deep mining shaft, the shallow workings, and the deep, open cuttings of the earlier times, and the stream works of the "old men." Thus we have on one spot a compendium of the history of mining for tin. Among the relics lying about are the remains of an old

CRAZING-MILL STONE, UPPER GOBBETTS.

crazing-mill, consisting of the upper and the nether stones. The nether stone is 3 feet 10 inches in diameter, and 10 inches thick. In the periphery is a groove forming a lip, that served readily to discharge the ground material.

The upper stone has a roughly convex back, and an eye as well as four holes drilled in it. Into these holes posts were fitted, which carried two bars, so that the stone was made to revolve by horse or man power, like the arrangement of a capstan.

The hole or eye of the nether stone was for the purpose of receiving a conical plug, the apex of which penetrated partly into the eye of the upper stone, and served the double purpose of keeping the runner stone in position and of distributing the feed equally on the grinding-surfaces.   To further assist

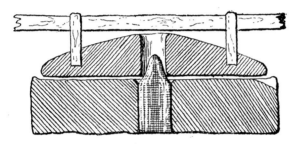

METHOD OF USING THE MILL-STONES.   SECTION.

this are four curved master-furrows or grooves, radiating from the eye of the grinding-surface of the upper stone.   The mill, worked by men or by horses, was of slow speed, and water was introduced to assist the propulsion of the ground material towards the grooved lip in the periphery of the stone.   This and the feed were, of course, introduced through the circular hole in the top stone.

On the site of what was evidently the blowing-house is a mould-stone, about 4 feet by 3.   The mould is 15 inches long by 11 inches wide at one end, and 10 inches at the other, and 4 to 5 inches deep. There are also cavities for sample ingots.

Other stones lie about with hollows worked in them, that seem to have been mortar-stones, used for pounding up the ore, at a period earlier than that at which the crazing-mill was introduced.

Further up the Swincombe, on the left, a little stream descends that has had its bed turned over and over. This is Deep Swincombe, and here are the remains of the earliest known smelting-house yet noticed on Dartmoor. It has been fully described in a previous chapter. On all sides we discover traces of those who in ancient times came to Dartmoor and toiled after metal. We go in swarms there now—to spend our metal and idle and gain health. So the old order changeth, and with it men's moods and manners.

To return to Holne. In the parsonage Charles Kingsley was born, but the house has since been to a large extent rebuilt. On a fly-sheet of the Book of Burial Registers is the entry, "The Vicarage House, being very *dilapidated*, was taken down and rebuilt by the Vicar (the Rev. John D. Parham) in the year 1832." It was in that "very dilapidated" house that Charles Kingsley was born.

A curious custom existed at Holne, now given up. There is, near the village, a "Ploy (play) Field" in which stood formerly a rude granite stone six or seven feet high.

On May morning, before daybreak, the young men of the village were wont to assemble there and then proceed to the moor, where they selected a ram lamb,

and, after running it down, brought it in triumph
to the Ploy Field, fastened it to the granite post, cut
its throat, and then roasted it whole—skin, wool, etc.
At midday a struggle took place, at the risk of cut
hands, for a slice, it being supposed to confer luck
for the ensuing year on the fortunate devourer. As
an act of gallantry the young men sometimes fought
their way through the crowd to get a slice for the
chosen amongst the young women, all of whom, in
their best dresses, attended the Ram Feast, as it
was called. Dancing, wrestling, and other games,
assisted by copious libations of cider during the
afternoon, prolonged the festivity till midnight. This
is now entirely of the past, but a somewhat similar
popular festival survives at King's Teignton, or did
so till recently. There Whitsuntide is the season
chosen. A lamb is drawn about the parish on
Whitsun Monday in a cart covered with garlands
of lilac, laburnum, and other flowers, when persons
are requested to give something towards the animal
and attendant expenses. On Tuesday morning it is
killed and roasted whole in the middle of the village.
The lamb is then sold in slices to the poor at a
cheap rate. The story told to account for this
festival is that the village once suffered from a
dearth of water, when the inhabitants were advised
to pray for water; whereupon a fountain burst forth
in a meadow about a third of a mile above the river,
in an estate now called Rydon, a supply sufficient
to meet the necessities of the villagers. A lamb,
it is said, has ever since been sacrificed as a return
offering at Whitsuntide in the manner above mentioned.

The said water appears like a large pond, from which in rainy weather may be seen jets springing up some inches above the surface in many parts.

I know the case of a farmer on the edge of Dartmoor, whose cattle were afflicted with some disorder in 1879; he thereupon conveyed a sheep to the ridge above his house, sacrificed and burnt it there, as an offering to the Pysgies. The cattle at once began to recover, and did well after, nor were there any fresh cases of sickness amongst them. Since then I have been told of other and very similar cases.

IVYBRIDGE

THIS not very interesting spot may be chosen as a centre whence the Avon, Erme, and Yealm river valleys may be explored. The distances are considerable, but the railway facilitates reaching starting-points—South Brent for the Avon, and Cornwood for the Yealm. It is advisable to ascend one river, cross a ridge, and descend another river.

The moors on this, the south, side are by no means so bold as are those on the other sides, but the valleys are hardly to be surpassed for beauty; and they give access to very remarkable groups of antiquities, the distance to some of which beyond inclosed land, and the absence of roads on this part of the moor has saved these latter from destruction.

In Ivybridge itself there is absolutely nothing worth seeing, but the churches of Ugborough. and Ermington richly deserve a visit; and there are

P 209

some old manor houses, as Fardell, Fillham, Slade, and Fowelscombe, that may be seen with interest. We will begin with the valley of the Avon.

South Brent is dominated by Brent Hill, that was formerly crowned with a chapel dedicated to S. Michael. The parish church, a foundation of S. Petrock, possessed a fine carved oak screen. The church has, however, been taken in hand by that iconoclast the "restorer," who has left it empty, swept and garnished—a thing of nakedness and a woe for ever. The screen—the one glory of the church—was cast forth into the graveyard, and there allowed to rot.

The Avon foams down from the moor through a contracted throat, affording scenes of great beauty in its ravine. It receives the Glazebrook some way below South Brent, and the Bala about the same distance above it.

The river has to be ascended for two miles and a half before Shipley Bridge is reached, and then the moor is in front of one, with Zeal Plains spread out, strewn with prehistoric settlements that have not as yet been properly investigated.

The Abbots' Way, a track from Buckfast to Tavistock, crosses the Avon at Huntingdon's Cross, a rude unchamfered stone four feet and a half high. It stands immediately within the forest bounds. The moors already traversed are the commons of Brent and Dean. The cross is romantically situated in a rocky basin, the rising ground about it covered with patches of heather, with here and there a granite boulder protruding through the turf.

"All around is still and silent, save the low murmuring of the waters as they run over their pebbly bed. The only signs of life are the furry inhabitants of the warren, and, perchance, a herd of Dartmoor ponies, wild as the country over which they roam, and a few sheep or cattle grazing on the slopes. The cross is surrounded by rushes, and a dilapidated wall—the warren enclosure—runs near it."*

The Abbots' Way may here be distinctly seen ascending the left bank of the Avon.

On Quick Beam Hill, over which the Abbots' Way climbs to reach the valley of the Erme, is another cross, concerning which something must be said, as it shows that not only educated and intelligent architects are iconoclasts, but also illiterate and stupid workmen.

There is a cairn that bears the name of Whitaburrow, and till the year 1847, erect on it in the centre stood an old grey moorstone cross. In that year a company was formed to extract naphtha from the peat, and its works were established near Shipley Bridge, to which the peat was conveyed from this spot in tram-waggons.

There being no place of shelter near, the labourers erected a house on the summit of the cairn, which measures one hundred and ninety feet in circumference, and requiring a large stone as a support for their chimney-breast, they knocked off the arms of the cross and employed the shaft for that purpose. The house has disappeared with the exception of the foundations and about three feet in height of walling,

---

* CROSSING, *Ancient Crosses of Dartmoor*, p. 15.

but the poor old maimed shaft stands there aloft, just as the poor old maimed church of South Brent stands on the river far below. Each has lost that which made it significant and beautiful, each mutilated by the stupidity of man.

The cross takes its name from Sir William Petre of Tor Brian, who possessed certain rights over Brent Moor. He was Secretary of State in four reigns—those of Henry VIII., Edward VI., Mary, and Elizabeth—and seems to have conformed to which-ever religion was favoured by the Sovereign, like the Vicar of Bray. He died in 1571, and was the ancestor of the present Lord Petre.

On Ugborough Moor, that adjoins, is a third cross, called that of Hobajohn, which is planted, singularly enough, in the midst of a stone row. This row starts on Butterdon Hill, above Ivybridge, and passes within a short distance of Sharp Tor. I have not seen it, but learn that it, like most other stone rows, starts from a cairn inclosed within upright stones. It must, if really a stone row, be something like three miles in length. The cross has also been mutilated, and lies prostrate.

A fourth cross, Spurle's or Pearl's Cross, on Ugborough Moor, has lost its shaft.

The Abbots' Way from Avon valley leads to the Erme valley, where Redlake enters it at a very interesting point. Here, at the junction of this feeder, is a well-preserved blowing-house, with its wheel-pit and with its tin-moulds lying in the ruins.

The whole of Erme Plains and the valley for three miles down is simply crowded with hut circles, pounds, and other remains. On the height above, Staldon Moor, is a stone row of really astounding length, of which something has been already said. It starts at the south end from a large circle, which formerly inclosed a cairn, and ·stretches away to the north, over hill and down dale, for two miles and a quarter, and terminates in a kistvaen. The stones are not large, but the row is fairly intact.

Due south of this, on the south side of the highest point of Stall Moor, Staldon Barrow, are two more stone rows, almost, but not quite, in a line. In the neighbourhood are many cairns and kistvaens. The stones here are larger. Taken together the rows run over 1,400 feet. They can be seen from Cornwood Station when the light is favourable.

Again another row on Burford Down, a continuation of the same moor, starts from a circle containing a kistvaen near Tristis Rock, and stretches away north to a wall and across an inclosed field, but here it has been sadly pillaged for the construction of the wall. It still runs 1,500 feet. The Erme valley has been much worked by streamers, and some of the mining operations have been carried on at a comparatively recent period.

By the side of a little lateral gully on the right hand in descending the river is a beehive hut among the streamers' mounds ; it is quite intact, and shelter may be taken in it from a passing storm. It is, however, not prehistoric, but is a miners' *cache*.

Another, also perfect, is a little further down, on the other side of the river before reaching Piles Wood.

Harford church, another foundation of S. Petrock, stands high. It contains nothing of interest except an altar tomb with brasses upon it, in memory of Thomas Williams, Speaker of the House of Commons, of the family of that name formerly resident at Stowford, in the parish. And in the second place, a monument to John and Agnes Prideaux, the parents of John Prideaux, Bishop of Worcester. This was set up by the latter in 1639.

Hall, not far from the church, was for some time the residence of the notorious Elizabeth Chudleigh, Duchess of Kingston, who was tried and condemned for bigamy. It was a hard case. She was born in 1726, and was the daughter of Colonel Thomas Chudleigh, who died when Elizabeth was quite a child. In 1744, when she was aged only eighteen, she visited her maternal aunt, Anne Hanmer, at Lainston, near Winchester, met at the Winchester Races Lieutenant Hervey, second son of Lord Hervey, and grandson of the Earl of Bristol, who was then aged twenty. He was invited to Lainston, and one night in a foolish frolic, at eleven o'clock, with the connivance, if not at the instigation, of Mrs. Hanmer, Elizabeth was married to Lieutenant Hervey by the rector in the little roofless ruin of a church. No registers were signed, and the bridegroom left in two days to rejoin his ship, and sailed for the West Indies.

She never after that received Lieutenant Hervey as her husband, and he instituted a suit in the Consistory Court of the Bishop of London for the jactitation of the marriage, and sentence was given in 1769 declaring that the marriage form gone through in 1744 was null and void. On the strength of this Elizabeth married the Duke of Kingston, March 8, 1769.

No attempt was made during the lifetime of the Duke to dispute the legality of the union ; neither he nor Elizabeth had the least doubt that the former marriage had been legally dissolved. But when the Duke left all his great fortune to Elizabeth, then his nephews were furious, and raked up against her the charge of bigamy, on the grounds that the sentence of the Consistory Court was invalid. She was tried in Westminster Hall before her peers in 1776, and the trial lasted five days.

The penalty for bigamy was death, but she could escape this sentence by claiming the benefit of a statute of William and Mary, which commuted death to branding in the hand and imprisonment. The peers found her guilty, but she escaped punishment by flying to the Continent, where she died in 1788.*

Harford Hall, where she resided, has about it no architectural features ; it never can have been other than a small mansion, and is now a mere farmhouse. The trees around it alone indicate that it was at one time a gentleman's seat.

If now we strike across Stall Moor to the Yealm we come on Yealm Steps, where the river falls over a mass of granite débris. Here are two blowing-

---

* I have told her story in full in *Historic Oddities and Strange Events.* Methuen and Co., 1889.

houses, one above the steps and the other below. The lower house on the eastern side of the stream is a mere heap of ruins with, however, the door-jamb standing and facing the north.* No wheel-pit is visible, but there are traces of a watercourse at a high level to the north-east of the hut. Near the entrance is a stone with one perfect mould in it, and another imperfect. A second mould-stone is lying near an angle in the eastern wall of the house. It has in it two moulds adjoining each other—one at a lower level than the other, and connected by a channel. The high-level cavity is 15 inches long, 8 inches wide, and 3 inches deep. At one end is a groove one inch deep, perpendicular, and running down the side of the mould three inches; that is, from top to bottom.

The low-level mould is 17 inches long, 12 inches wide, and 5 inches deep. These cavities have been used for the purification of tin, for the molten metal mixed with furnace impurities poured in on the high-level hollow would flow in a purer condition into the low-level mould.

This blowing-house has been excavated, somewhat superficially, but nothing was found in it to give token of the period to which it belonged. About a quarter of a mile further up the river, but on the western bank, is another ruin. The doorway, which is very imperfect, is on the eastern side. One mould-stone remains, containing a mould 17 inches long, 12 inches wide, and from 4 to 5 inches deep.

* This is the scene chosen by me for my story *Guavas the Tinner*.

The whole slope of Stall Moor towards the south is strewn with hut circles, and between the Yealm and Broadall Lake is a pound containing several. On the further side of the stream is another pound, at which begins a singular wall that extends for over three miles as far as the Plym at Trowlesworthy Warren. For what purpose this wall was erected—whether as a boundary, or whether for defence—cannot be determined. It is in connection with several pounds and clusters of hut circles.

In the valley of Hawns and Dendles is a pretty cascade, a great haunt of the tripper, who ravages the Yealm valley and tears up and carries off the ferns and roots of wild flowers.

A few instances of the habits of the tripper may not seem amiss, as exhibited in the Yealm valley.

Blachford was the residence of the late Lord Blachford, the friend of Gladstone.

One day my lady saw a woman—a. tripper—in front of the house, where there is a rockery, tearing up ferns. Lady Blachford rushed forth to interfere.

"Oh!" said the tripper, "I only did it so as to get a sight of Lord Blachford. I thought if I executed some mischief I might draw him forth."

A peculiarly fine rhododendron grew in front of the vicarage. It attracted the tripper by its beautiful masses of flower. One evening an individual of this not uncommon species proceeded to tear it up, assisted by trowel and knife; and finally having hacked through the roots, carried it off; but finding the load burdensome at the first hill, threw it away.

A gentleman residing further down the valley was

cultivating a rare flowering shrub. After seven years it put forth its tassels of bloom. He tarried a day or two before gathering the blossoms till they were fully out. His wife was an invalid, and he purposed showing them to her when in their full perfection. But before he carried his purpose into execution, he went to Cornwood Station to meet a friend, when he perceived a "lady" on the platform with her hands full of the flowers. He approached her and civilly inquired where she had obtained the beautiful bunches.

"Oh! they were growing in Mr. P.'s ground, so I went in and gathered them. I know Mr. P. well, and I am convinced he would not object."

"You have the advantage of me, madam. I am Mr. P. But to a lady, as to a Christian, all things are lawful, though all things may not be expedient."

A friend threw open his grounds to a great party of school teachers and their scholars. The neighbourhood had been denuded of the *Osmunda regalis* by the tripper, but the beautiful fern had a sanctuary in his preserves. However, the visitors dug up, tore away, and destroyed his plants wholesale, and returned to town burdened with the wreckage. The *Osmunda* is a slow grower, and takes many years to reach maturity.

So much for the tripper. I do not in the least suppose any of this race will see more of my book than the outside. But I write this for the intelligent visitor, to warn him against Hawns and Dendles on Plymouth early closing day (Wednesday) in summer.

Wisdome is the ancestral house of the Rogers family, of which the late Lord Blachford was the representative. It is a modest, picturesque old moorland mansion of a small gentle family. Slade, on the other hand, must have been a house of consequence ; it still possesses a noble hall, with richly carved oak wainscotting. Steart has handsome carved armorial gates ; and Fardell is remarkable as a home of the Raleigh family, and had its licensed chapel. The grandfather of the navigator lived at Fardell, and Sir Walter himself was probably there much in his early days. Here was found an ogham inscription on a stone, now in the British Museum, which shows that the Irish had conquered and colonised Devon as far south as Cornwood. Other oghams have been found at Tavistock, and at Lewannick, near Launceston.

According to local belief, the stone indicated where treasure was hid ; and a jingle was current in the neighbourhood :—

> " Between this stone and Fardell Hall
> Lies as much money as the devil can haul."

The stone bore the inscription, " Fanonii Macquisini " on one side, and " Sapanni " on the other. The " Mac " in the name is conclusively Irish, as also the oghams.

CHAPTER XV.

YELVERTON

YELVERTON is a corruption of Elford-town.
The mansion near the station was formerly a
seat of the Elfords of Sheeps Tor. The family is
now extinct, at least in the neighbourhood where
at one time it was of dignity and well estated.
Yelverton is itself a mere collection of villa residences of Plymouth men of business, but it forms
a convenient point of departure for many interesting
expeditions.

The principal residence of the Elfords was at
Longstone, in Sheeps Tor, where the old house
remains little altered, and where the *windstrew*
should be seen, a granite platform, raised above the
field, on which thrashing could be carried on by
the aid of the winds that carried away the chaff.

The tor which gives its name to the village and
parish stands by itself, and rises to about 1,200 feet.

THE DEWERSTONE

It is a picturesque hill, and only needs the addition of another couple of hundred put to its elevation to make it perfect.

The basin below the village was anciently a lake, the water being retained by a barrier of rock where stands now the dam for the reservoir. This, in time, was silted up to the depth of ninety feet, and now the Plymouth Corporation, by the construction of a fine and eminently picturesque barrier across the narrow gorge through which the Meavy flows, have reconverted this basin into a lake.

Near the summit of the tor is the Pixy Cave, in which Squire Elford remained concealed whilst the Roundheads searched Longstone for him. Some faithful tenants in the village kept him supplied with food till pursuit was at an end. The Elfords inherited Longstone from the Scudamores at the close of the fifteenth century. The parish was then called Shettes Tor, from the Celtic *syth*, steep; but the name has been altered in this or last century. The last Elford of Sheeps Tor was John, who married Admonition Prideaux, and died without issue in 1748, his six children having predeceased him. A side branch of the family—to which, however, Sheeps Tor did not fall—produced Sir William Elford, Bart., of Bickham, but he died in 1837, without male issue, and the title became extinct. His monument is in Totnes church.

A man named Cole, working at the granite quarries at Merrivale Bridge, a few years ago sang me a song concerning a doe that escaped from Elford Park, which was probably situated where is now Yelverton.

THE SILLY DOE

˙Give ear unto my mournful song
　　Gay huntsmen every one,
And unto you I will relate
　　My sad and doleful moan.
O here I be a silly Doe,
　　From Elford Park I strayed,
In leaving of my company
　　Myself to death betrayed.

The master said I must be slain
　　For 'scaping from his bounds :
" O keeper, wind the hunting horn,
　　And chase him with your hounds."
A Duke of royal blood was there,
　　And hounds of noble race ;
They gathered in a rout next day,
　　And after me gave chase.

They roused me up one winter morn,
　　The frost it cut my feet,
My red, red blood came trickling down,
　　And made the scent lie sweet.
For many a mile they did me run,
　　Before the sun went down,
Then I was brought to give a teen,
　　And fall upon the groun'.

The first rode up, it was the Duke :
　　Said he, " I'll have my will ! "
A blade from out his belt he drew
　　My sweet red blood to spill.
So with good cheer they murdered me,
　　As I lay on the ground ;
My harmless life it bled away,
　　Brave huntsmen cheering round.

I am a little puzzled as to whether the dry sarcasm in this song is intentional.* The melody is peculiarly sweet and plaintive. *When* a royal duke hunted last on Dartmoor I have been unable to ascertain.

The red deer were anciently common on Dartmoor. It was not till King John's reign that Devon was disafforested, with the exception of Dartmoor and Exmoor. But the deer were mischievous to the crops of the farmer, and to the young plantations, and farmers, yeomen, and squires combined to get rid of them from Dartmoor. Still, however, occasionally one runs from Exmoor and takes refuge in the woods about the Dart, the Plym, and the Tavy.

But it is for fox, hare, and otter hunting that the sportsman goes to Dartmoor, and not for the deer. A very pretty sight it is to see a pack with the scarlet coats after it sweeping over the moorside in pursuit of Reynard, and to hear the music of the hounds and horns.

For the harriers the great week is that after hare-hunting is at an end in the lowlands or "in-country." Then the several packs that have hunted through the season on the circumference of the moor unite on it, and take turns through the week on the moor itself. The great day of that week is Bellever Day, when the meet is on the tor of that name. I have described it in my *Book of the West*, and will not repeat what has been already related. But I will venture to quote an account of otter-hunting on the Dart from the pen of Mr. William Collier, than whom no one

* I have given it, with the original air, in the *Garland of Country Song*. Methuen.

has been more of an enthusiast for sport on the moor.

"The West Dart is the perfection of a Dartmoor river, flowing bright and rapid over a bed of granite boulders richly covered with moss and lichen, its banks bedecked with ferns and wild flowers of the moor, and fringed with the bog-myrtle and withy.

"Water holds scent well, and the whiff so fragrant to the nose of the hound rises to the surface and floats down stream, calling forth his musical chant of praise. For this reason otter-hunters draw up stream, and before the lair of the otter is reached the welkin rings with the music of the pack. The otter has left his trail on the banks, and on the stones where he has landed when fishing, his spoor can be seen freshly printed on a sandy nook, and he is very likely to be found in a well-known and remarkably safe holt, as they call it in the West, about half a mile above Dart Meet, which he shares at times with foxes, though his access to it is under water, and theirs, of course, above. If he were but wise enough to stay there he might defy his legitimate enemies to do their worst. But he knows not man or his little ways, and he has heard the unwonted strain of the hounds as they have been crying over his footsteps hard by. They mark him in his retreat, and the whole pack proclaim that he is in the otter's parlour, the strongest place on the river. It is in a large rock hanging over a deep, dark pool, in a corner made by a turn in the river, with an old battered oak tree growing somehow from the midst, and backed by a confused jumble of granite blocks. The artist and the fisherman both admire this spot, though for totally different reasons, but the hunter likes it not, for he knows too well that if he runs the fox or the otter here his sport is over. A fox or an otter if run here is likely to

SHEEPS TOR

stay; he has experienced the dangers and wickedness of
the world at large; but if found here in his quiet and
repose he takes alarm at the unusual turmoil, and incon-
tinently bolts.   The otter is known to have a way in under
water, where no terrier can go, and he is so far safer than
the fox.   The most arduous otter-hunters, therefore, when
the hounds mark, plunge up to their necks in the water to
frighten him out with their otter-poles.   He has long known
the Dart as a quiet, peaceable, happy hunting-ground; and
he makes the fatal mistake of bolting, little recking what a
harrying awaits him for the next four hours.   There immediately arises a yell of 'Hoo-gaze!' the view halloo of
the otter-hunter, probably an older English hunting halloo
than 'Tally ho!' and the din of the hounds and terriers, the
human scream, and the horn, like Bedlam broken loose,
which he hears behind him, make him hurry up-stream as
best he may.   The master of the hounds, if he knows his
business, will now call for silence, and, taking out his
watch, will give the otter what he calls a quarter of an
hour's law.   It is wonderful how fond sportsmen are of
law; perhaps there is an affinity between prosecuting
a case and pursuing a chase.   He wants the otter to go
well away from his parlour, and his object for the rest of
the day will be to keep him out of it.   If he is a real
good sporting otter-hunter he will tell his field that he
wants his hounds to kill the otter without assistance from
them; for in the West of England the vice of mobbing
the otter is too common, with half the field in the water,
hooting, yelling, poking with otter-poles, mixing the wrong
scent (their own) with the right, making the water muddy,
and turning the river into a brawling brook with a ven-
geance.   The true otter-hunter only wants his huntsman
and whip, and perhaps a very knowing and trustworthy
friend, besides himself, to help in hunting the otter *with*

Q

his hounds, and not with men. The master gives the chase
a good quarter of an hour by the clock; and, leaving the
unearthly, or perhaps too earthly sounds behind him, the
otter makes up-stream as fast as he can go. It is surprising
how far an otter can get in the time, but fear lends speed
to his feet. Then begins the prettiest part of the sport.
The hounds are laid on, they dash into the river, and
instantly open in full cry. The water teems with the scent
of the otter; but the deep pools, rapid stickles, and rocky
boulders over which the river foams hinder the pace. There
is ample time to admire the spirit-stirring and beautiful
scene. The whole pack swimming a black-looking pool
under a beetling tor in full chorus; now and then an en-
couraging note on the horn; the echoes of the deep valley;
the foaming and roaring Dart flowing down from above;
the rich colour from the fern, the gorse, the heather, the
moss, and the wild flowers; a few scattered weather-beaten
oaks and fir trees, and the stately tors aloft, striking on the
eye and ear, make one feel that otter-hunting on Dartmoor
is indeed a sport.

"The Dart is a large river, for a Dartmoor stream, and
presents many obstacles to the hounds; but they pursue
the chase for some distance, and at length stop and mark,
as they did before. The otter has got out of hearing, and
has rested in a lair known to him under the river-bank.
The terriers and an otter-pole dislodge him, and the sport
becomes fast and furious. He is seen in all directions,
sometimes apparently in two places at once, which makes
the novice think there are two or three otters afoot.
'Hoo-gaze!' is now often heard, as one or another
catches sight of him, and the field become very noisy
and excited. It is still the object to run him up-stream,
whilst he now finds it easier to swim down. 'Look out
below!' is therefore heard in the fine voice of the master.

There is a trusty person down-stream watching a shallow stickle, where the otter must be seen if he passes. Suddenly the clamour ceases, and silence prevails. The otter has mysteriously disappeared, and he has to be fresh found. The master is in no hurry. There is too much scent in the water of various sorts, and he will be glad to pause till it has floated away. He takes his hounds down-stream. The trusty man says the otter has not passed; but this makes no difference. Some way further down, with a wave of his hand, he sends all the hounds into the river again with a dash. They draw up-stream again, pass the trusty man still at his post, and reach the spot where the otter vanished. The river is beautifully clear again, and an old hound marks. A good hour, perhaps, has been lost, or rather spent, since the otter disappeared, and here he has been in one of his under-water dry beds. He is routed out by otter-poles, and liveliness again prevails, especially when he takes to the land to get down-stream by cutting off a sharp curve in the river—a way he has learnt in his frogging expeditions—and the hounds run him then like a fox. He is only too glad to plunge headlong into the river again, and he has reached it below the trusty man, who, however, goes down to the next shallow, and takes with him some others to turn the otter up from his safe parlour. They are hunting him now in a long deep pool, where he shifts from bank to bank, moving under water whilst the hounds swim above. He has a large supply of air in his lungs, which he vents as he uses it, and which floats to the surface in a series of bubbles. Otter-hunters calls it his chain, and it follows him wherever he goes, betraying his track in the muddiest water. He craftily puts his nose, his nose only, up to get a fresh supply of air now and then, under a bush or behind a rock, and then owners of sharp eyes call 'Hoo-gaze!' He finds himself in desperate straits, and he makes up his mind to go for his parlour at all hazards ; but the hounds catch sight of him in the shallow of the trusty man, and the chase comes to an end. Otters are never speared in the West." *

And now to return to Sheeps Tor and the picturesque village that nestles under it.

The one building-stone is granite, grey and soft of tone. The village is small, and consists of a few cottages about the open space before the church.

This latter is of the usual moorland type, and in the Perpendicular style. Observe above the porch the curious carved stone, formerly forming part of a sun-dial, and dated 1640. It represents wheat growing out of a skull, and bears the inscription—

" Mors janua vitæ."

This church has most unfortunately been vulgarised internally. It once possessed not only a magnificent roodscreen, rich with gold and colour, but also a fifteenth-century carved pulpit that matched with the screen. The church was delivered over to a Tavistock builder to make watertight, as cheaply as might be, and he succeeded triumphantly in transforming what was once a treasury of art into a desolation. A few poor fragments of the screen have been set up in the church by the vicar, with an appeal to visitors to do something to obliterate the infamy of its destruction by a restoration out of what little remains. Most fortunately, working

* Slightly curtailed from W. F. COLLIER, *Country Matters in Short.* Duckworth, London, 1899.

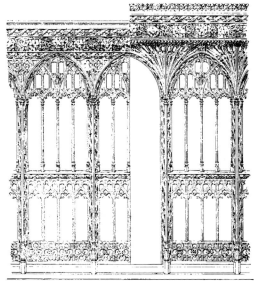

✣ROOD SCREEN✣SHEEPSTOR CHURCH✣
✣SOUTH DEVON✣

HALF SHEWING SCREEN AS
EXISTING PREVIOUS TO ITS DEMOLITION.

HALF SHEWING
CONJECTURAL RESTORATION.

PORTION OF SCREEN, SHEEPS TOR

drawings were taken of the screen before its destruction. I give not only a drawing to scale of a bay as it was, but also of a bay as it should be if restored, for the vaulting had disappeared before its final ruin and removal. Near the church stood formerly the old vicarage, a mediæval dwelling, intact, with its oak, nail-studded door and its panelled walls. This also has been destroyed.

What of old times still remains is the bull-ring to the south-east of the church. On the churchyard wall sat the principal parishioners, as in a dress circle. Near by is S. Leonard's Well, but it possesses no architectural interest.

In Burra Tor Wood is a pretty waterfall. Burra Tor was the residence of Rajah Brooke when in England. It had been presented to him by the Baroness Burdett Coutts and other admirers. In Sheeps Tor churchyard he lies, but Burra Tor has been sold since his death.

Above the wood stands Roman's Cross, probably called after S. Rumon or Ruan, whose body lay at Tavistock. There is another Rumon's Cross on Lee Moor.

The drive from Douseland round Yennadon, above the dam and the reservoir, to Sheeps Tor village, is hardly to be surpassed for beauty anywhere on the moor.

A walk that will richly repay the pedestrian is one up the valley of the Narra Tor Brook, between Sheeps Tor and Down Tor. He follows the Devonport leat till he reaches the turn on the right to Nosworthy Bridge. He passes Vinneylake, where

are two interesting *caches*, one cut out of the con-
glomerate rubble brought down from the decomposed
rocks above. This is now used as a turnip-house, but
it is to be suspected it was anciently employed as a
private still-house. In a field hard by is another,
more like some of the Cornish structural fogous. It
is roofed over with slabs of granite.

The ascent of Deancombe presents many peeps of
great beauty. At the farm the road comes to an
end, and here the tor must be ascended. East of
Down Tor is a very fine stone row, starting from a
circle of stones inclosing a cairn, and extending in
the direction of a large, much-disturbed cairn. There
is a blocking-stone at the eastern end, and a menhir
by the ring of stones at the west end of the row.
The length is 1,175 feet.

I visited this row with the late Mr. Lukis in 1880,
when we found that men had been recently engaged
on the row with crowbars. They had thrown down
the two largest stones at the head. We appealed to
Sir Massey Lopes, and he stopped the destruction of
the monument, and since then Mr. R. Burnard and I
have re-erected the stones then thrown down.

On the slope of Coombshead Tor are numerous
hut circles and a pound.

From the stone row a walk along the ridge of the
moor leads to Nun's Cross. This bore on it the
inscription, " CRUX SIWARDI." It is very rude ; it
stands 7 feet 4 inches high, and is fixed in a socket
cut in a block of stone sunk in the ground. It was
overthrown and broken about 1846, but was restored
by the late Sir Ralph Lopes. By whom and for what

ON THE MEAVY

cause it was overthrown never transpired. The inscription with the name of Siward is now difficult to decipher. On the other side of the cross is "BOC—LOND"—three letters forming one line, and the remaining four another, directly under it. The cross is alluded to in a deed of 1240 as then standing.

Nun's Cross is probably a corruption of Nant Cross, the cross at the head of the *nant* or valley. The whole of Newleycombe Lake has been extensively streamed. The hill to the north is dense with relics of an ancient people. Roundy Farm, now in ruins, takes its name from the pounds which contributed to form the walls of its inclosures, many of which follow the old circular erections that once inclosed a primeval village. The ruined farmhouse bears the initials of a Crymes, a family once as great as that of the Elfords, but now gone. It is interesting to know that the farmer's wife of Kingset, that now includes Roundy Farm, was herself a Crymes. One very perfect hut circle here was for long used as a potato garden.

Hard by is Clakeywell Pool, by some called Crazywell. It is an old mine-work, now filled with water. It covers nearly an acre, and the banks are in part a hundred feet high. According to popular belief, at certain times at night a loud voice is heard calling from the water in articulate tones, naming the next person who is to die in the parish. At other times what are heard are howls as of a spirit in torment. The sounds are doubtless caused by a swirl of wind in the basin that contains the pond. An old lady, now deceased, told me how that as a child she dreaded going near this tarn—she lived at Shaugh—fearing lest she should hear the voice calling her by name.

The idea of mysterious voices is a very old one. The schoolboy will recall the words of Virgil in the first *Georgic :—*

> "Vox . . . per lucos vulgo exaudita silentes
> Ingens."

The "wisht hounds" that sweep overhead in the dark barking are brentgeese going north or returning south. They have given occasion to many stories of strange voices in the sky.

In Ceylon the devil-bird has been the source of much superstitious terror.

A friend who has long lived in Ceylon says: "Never shall I forget when first I heard it. I was at dinner, when suddenly the wildest, most agonised shrieks pierced my ear. I was under the impression that a woman was being murdered outside my house. I snatched up a cudgel and ran forth to her aid, but saw no one." The natives regard this cry of the mysterious devil-bird with the utmost fear. They believe that to hear it is a sure presage of death ; and they are not wrong. When they have heard it, they pine to death, killed by their own conviction that life is impossible.

Autenrieth, professor and physician at Tübingen, in 1822 published a treatise on *Aërial Voices*, in which he collected a number of strange accounts of mysterious sounds heard in the sky, and which he

thought could not all be deduced from the cries of
birds at night.   He thus generalises the sounds :—

"They are heard sometimes flying in this direction, then
in the opposite through the air; mostly, they are heard as
though coming down out of the sky; but at other times as
if rising from the ground.   They resemble occasionally
various musical instruments; occasionally also the clash of
arms, or the rattle of drums, or the blare of trumpets.
Sometimes they are like the tramp of horses, or the discharge of distant artillery.   But sometimes, also, they consist in an indescribably hollow, thrilling, sudden scream.
Very commonly they resemble all kinds of animal tones,
mostly the barking of dogs.   Quite as often they consist
in a loud call, so that the startled hearer believes himself
to be called by name, and to hear articulate words addressed to him.   In some instances, Greeks have believed
they were spoken to in the language of Hellas, whereas
Romans supposed they were addressed in Latin.   The
modern Highlanders distinctly hear their vernacular Gaelic.
These aërial voices accordingly are so various that they
can be interpreted differently, according to the language
of the hearer, or his inner conception of what they might
say."

The Jews call the mysterious voice that falls from
the heaven Bathkol, and have many traditions relative to it.   The sound of arms and of drums and
artillery may safely be set down to the real vibrations
of arms, drums, and artillery at a great distance,
carried by the wind.

In the desert of Gobi, which divides the moun-
tainous snow-clad plateau of Thibet from the milder
regions of Asia, travellers assert that they have heard

sounds high up in the sky as of the clash of arms or of musical martial instruments. If travellers fall to the rear or get separated from the caravan, they hear themselves called by name. If they go after the voice that summons them, they lose themselves in the desert. Sometimes they hear the tramp of horses, and taking it for that of their caravan, are drawn away, and wander from the right course and become hopelessly lost. The old Venetian traveller Marco Polo mentions these mysterious sounds, and says that they are produced by the spirits that haunt the desert. They are, however, otherwise explicable. On a vast plain the ear loses the faculty of judging direction and distance of sounds; it fails to possess, so to speak, acoustic perspective. When a man has dropped away from the caravan, his comrades call to him; but he cannot distinguish the direction whence their voices come, and he goes astray after them.

Rubruquis, whom Louis IX. sent in 1253 to the court of Mongu-Khan, the Mongol chief, says that in the Altai Mountains, that fringe the desert of Gobi, demons try to lure travellers astray. As he was riding among them one evening with his Mongol guide, he was exhorted by the latter to pray, because otherwise mishaps might occur through the demons that haunted the mountains luring them out of the right road.

Morier, the Persian traveller, at the beginning of this century speaks of the salt desert near Khom. On it, he says, travellers are led astray by the cry of the goblin Ghul, who, when he has enticed them from the road, rends them with his claws. Russian accounts of Kiev in the beginning of the nineteenth century mention an island lying in a salt marsh between the Caspian and the Aral Sea, where, in the evening, loud sounds are heard like the baying of hounds, and hideous cries as well; consequently the island is reputed to be haunted, and no one ventures near it.

That the Irish banshee may be traced to an owl admits of little doubt; the description of the cries so closely resembles what is familiar to those who live in an owl-haunted district, as to make the identification all but certain. Owls are capricious birds. One can never calculate on them for hooting. Weeks will elapse without their letting their notes be heard, and then all at once for a night or two they will be audible, and again become silent—even for months.

The river Dart is said to cry. The sound is a peculiarly weird one; it is heard only when the wind is blowing down its deep valley, and is produced by the compression of the air in the winding passage. Whether it is calling for its annual tribute of a human life, I do not know, but of the river it is said :—

> "The Dart, the Dart—the cruel Dart
> Every year demands a heart!"

To return to our walk.

If the path be taken leading back to Nosworthy Bridge, beside and in the road will be seen several mould-stones for tin.

Leather Tor is a fine pile of ruined granite. I

have been informed that great quantities of flints have been found there, showing that at this spot there was a manufacturing of silex weapons and tools.

From Sheeps Tor the Drizzlecombe remains are reached with great ease. Here, near a tributary of the Plym, are three stone rows and two fine menhirs, a kistvaen, a large tumulus, and beside the stream a blowing-house with its mould-stones. Two of the rows are single, but one is double for a portion of its length only. There are blocking-stones and menhirs to each. The row connected with the great menhir is 260 feet long.

Sheeps Tor has been brought into the world by the construction of the reservoir. Formerly it was a place very much left to itself. There the old fiddler hung on who played venerable tunes, to which the people danced their old country dances. These latter may still be seen there, but, alas! the aged fiddler is dead. At one time it was a great musical centre, and it was asserted that two-thirds of the male population were in the church choir, acting either as singers or as instrumentalists.

We will now turn our steps towards Meavy.

Here is a house that belonged to the Drake family, half pulled down, a village cross under a very ancient oak, and a church in good condition.

There is some very early rude carving at the chancel arch in a pink stone, whence derived has not been ascertained.

Marchant's Cross is at the foot of the steep ascent to Ringmoor Down. It is the tallest of all the moor crosses, being no less than 8 feet 2 inches in height.

Another cross is in the hedge on Lynch Common.

Trowlesworthy Warren is situated among hut circles and inclosures. There is a double stone row on the southern slope, but it has been sadly

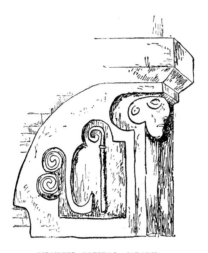

CHANCEL CAPITAL, MEAVY.

mutilated. The whole of the neighbouring moors are strewn with primeval habitations.

On Lee Moor and Headon Down may be seen the production of kaolin.

William Cookworthy, born at Kingsbridge in Devon, in 1705, was one of a large family. His father lost all his property in South Sea stock, and died leaving his widow to rear the children as best she might. They were Quakers, and help was forthcoming from the Friends. William kept his eyes about him, and discovered the china-clay which is found to so large an extent in Devon and Cornwall, and he laid the foundation of the kaolin trade between 1745 and 1750. One of the first places where he identified the clay was on Tregonning Hill in S. Breage parish, Cornwall, and to his dying day he was unaware of the enormous deposits on Lee Moor close to his Plymouth home.

He took out a patent in 1768 for the manufacture of Plymouth china, specimens of which are now eagerly sought after.

Kaolin is dissolved feldspar, deposited from the granite which has yielded to atmospheric and aqueous influences.

The white clay is dug out of pits and then is washed in tanks, in which the clayey sediment is collected. This sediment has, however, first to be purged of much of its mica and coarser particles as the stream in which it is dissolved is conveyed slowly over shallow "launders."

At the bottom of the pits are plugs, and so soon as the settled kaolin is sufficiently thick, these plugs are withdrawn, and the clay, now of the consistency of treacle, is allowed to flow into tanks at a lower level. Here it remains for three weeks or a month to thicken, when it is transferred to the "dry," a long shed with a well-ventilated roof, and with a furnace at one end and flues connected with it that traverse the whole "dry" and discharge into a chimney at the further end of the building. On the floor of this shed the clay rapidly dries, and it is then removed in spadefuls and packed in barrels or bags, or merely tossed into trucks for lading vessels. The clay is now white as snow, and is employed either in the Staffordshire potteries for the manufacture of porcelain, or else for bleaching—that is to say, for thickening calicoes, and for putting a surface on paper. Some is employed in the manufacture of alum; a good deal goes to Paris to be served up as the white sugar of confectionery, and it is hinted that not a little is employed in the adulteration of flour. America, as well, imports it for the manufacture of artificial teeth.

Great heaps of white refuse will be seen about the china-clay works; these are composed of the granitic sandy residuum. Of this there are several qualities, and it is sold to plasterers and masons, and the coarsest is gladly purchased for gravelling garden walks. The water that flows from the clay works is white as milk, and has a peculiar sweet taste. Cows are said to drink it with avidity. The full pans in drying present a metallic blue or green glaze on the surface.

The kaolin sent to Staffordshire travels by boat from Plymouth to Runcorn, where it is transhipped on to barges on the Bridgewater Canal, and is so conveyed to the belt of pottery towns, Burslem, Hanley, Stoke, and Longton.

The Dewerstone towers up at the junction of the Meavy and the Plym. On the side of the Plym there are sheer precipices of granite standing up as church spires above the brawling river. The face towards the Meavy is less abrupt, and it is on this side that an ascent can be made, but it is a scramble.

On reaching the top, it will be seen that the headland has been fortified by a double rampart of stone thrown across the neck of land. Wigford Down is in the rear, with kistvaens and tumuli and hut circles on it.

The visitor should descend in the direction of Goodameavy, and thence follow down the river that abounds in beautiful scenes. It was formerly believed that a wild hunter appeared on the summit of Dewerstone, attended by his black dogs, blowing a horn. From Dewerstone the visitor may walk to Bickleigh Station, and take the train for Tavistock, which I have written about in my *Book of the West*, and will not re-describe in the present work.

POST BRIDGE

A COLONY about a school-chapel and a few deformed beech trees in a basin among tors constitute Post Bridge.

Here the East Dart flows through a filled-up lake-bed, and passes away by a narrow cleft that it has sawn for itself through the granite.

The beech trees were planted at the same time that two lodges were erected by a gentleman called Hullett, who was induced to believe that he could convert a portion of Dartmoor into paradise. He purposed building a mansion at Stannon, and actually began the house. But by the time the lodges were set up and a wing of his house, he had discovered that Dartmoor would spell ruin, and he threw up his attempt. And Dartmoor will spell ruin unless approached and treated in the only suitable manner. It will pasture cattle and feed ponies and sheep, but it will never grow corn and roots.

The great central causeway crossed the modern road near the Dissenting chapel, and may be traced in the marsh aiming for the river, beyond which it ascends the hill and strikes along the brow behind Archerton. It is paved, and is a continuation of the old Fosse Way. It is certainly not Roman work, but British.

Post Bridge has been termed, not accurately, a prehistoric metropolis of the moor. This is because round the ancient lake-bed were numerous pounds containing hut circles. Most of these have now been destroyed, yet one remains perfect—Broadun; and adjoining it is Broadun Ring, where the outer circle of the inclosure has been pulled down, but a considerable number of the huts has been spared. There remain indications of fifteen of these inclosures. More have certainly been destroyed.

Lake-head Hill has been almost denuded of the monuments that once crowded it. They were systematically removed by the farmer at Bellever. Happily one kistvaen has been left on the summit, and there are two or three others, small and ruinous, on the sides.

The "cyclopean bridge" over the Dart is composed of rude masses of granite maintained in position by their own weight. It was the old packhorse bridge.

There are other bridges of the same description; one is on the stream at Bellever, one under Bairdown. But a structure of this sort is the simplest and most easily reared on Dartmoor, where lime is not found, and has to be brought at great expense from a distance.

Great numbers of worked flints are found in this neighbourhood, and a bronze ferrule to a spear was dug up a few years ago in Gawlor Bottom.

A little way, but a few steps below the bridge, on the west side, is a comparatively modern blowing-house; two mould-stones for tin may be seen there lying among the nettles. This house is built with mortar and is of considerable size, whereas the ancient blowing-houses are very small, and no lime has been employed in their construction. One of these with a *cache* may be found in the midst of the tinners' heaps if the Dart be followed up to where it makes a sudden bend and comes from the east. Here a tongue of hill stands out above it, and a stream sweeps down from the north to join it. A very short distance up this stream is the blowing-house with a beehive *cache*.

If this stream be pursued, and Sittaford Tor be aimed at, then a few hundred yards to the right of the tor the Grey Wethers will be found, two very fine circles in contact with one another; but the stones of one are nearly all down.

If the Ordnance Sheet XCIX., N.W., be taken, and the ridge followed north-west along the line indicated by bench-marks, Cut Hill will finally be attained, which is all bog, but which has a gash cut in it to afford a passage through the moors from Okehampton to Post Bridge. This expedition will take the visitor into some of the wildest and most desolate portions of the northern half of Dartmoor.

Many years ago the question was mooted in, I think, the *Times*, whether there were really such things as Jack-o'-lanterns.

Few instances can be recorded where this *ignis fatuus* has been seen on Dartmoor, probably because so few cattle are lost in the bogs there. I was told by a man accustomed to draw turf, that he has seen the legs and belly of the horse as though on fire, where it had been splashed by the peat water.

I walked one night from Plymouth to Tavistock across Roborough Down, before it was inclosed and built upon, and I then saw a little blue flame dancing on a pool. I went on my knees and crept close to it, to make quite sure what it was, and that it was not a glow-worm.

Mr. Coaker, of Sherberton, informs me that he has on several occasions seen the Jack-o'-lantern. There is a bit of marshy land where rises Muddy Lake, near the road from Princetown to Ashburton, and he has seen it there. Sometimes, according to his account, it appears like the flash of a lantern, and then disappears, and presently flashes again. It has also been seen by him in the boggy ground of Slade by Huccaby Bridge. There, on one occasion, he made his way towards it. From a distance the light seemed to be considerable, but as he approached it appeared only as a small flame.

The Rev. T. E. Fox, curate, living at Post Bridge, and serving the little chapel there and that at Huccaby, has also seen it, in Brimpts, hovering, a greenish-blue flame, about three feet above the soil; and a woman living near informs me that she also has noticed it in the same place.*

---

* I have been informed that the Jack-o'-lantern is only to be seen after a hot summer, at the end of July, and in August and September. As the moormen say, "When the vaen rises," *i.e.* when there is fermentation going on in the fen or vaen.

LAKEHEAD, KISTAVEN

The reader must excuse me if I tell the tales just as told to me, and mix up facts with what I consider fictions. I cannot doubt that these lights have been seen by others as well as by myself, and I am not surprised if here and there some superstition has attached itself to these phenomena.

The following story is told in the parish of Broadwoodwidger, where is a field in which, it is asserted, Will-o'-the-wisp is seen.

The farmer's son was delicate, and in haymaking time assisted in the work, and I have no doubt, notwithstanding his feeble lungs, in making sweet hay with the maidens. However, he over-exerted himself, broke a blood-vessel, and died. Ever since a blue flame has been seen dancing in this field, and even on the top of the haycocks.

The tale I have heard told, as a child, of a blue flame being seen leaving the churchyard and travelling down the lanes or roads to a certain door, and there waiting and returning accompanied by another flame, which appeared simultaneously with a death occurring in the house, is doubtless a distortion of a fact that such a flame as the Jack-o'-lantern *does* occasionally appear in graveyards.

A miner engaged at the Whiteworks crossed the moor on a Saturday to Cornwood, to see a brother who was dangerously ill, and started to return somewhat late on the Sunday afternoon. In consequence, night overtook him on the moor; he became entangled among the bogs, and was in sore distress, unable to proceed or to retreat.

Being an eminently God-fearing man, he took off his cap and prayed.

All at once a little light sprang up and moved forward. He knew that this was a Will-o'-the-wisp, and that it was held to lead into dangerous places; but his confidence in Providence was so strong, and so assured was he that the light was sent in answer to his prayer, that he followed it. He was conducted over ground fairly firm, though miry, till he reached heather and a sound footing, whereupon the flame vanished. Thanking God, he pursued his way, taking his direction by the stars, and reached his destination in safety.

"I tell the tale as 'twas told to me," but I will not vouch for the truth of it, as I did not hear it from the man himself, nor did I know him personally, so as to judge whether his word could be trusted.

Here, however, is an instance on which implicit reliance can be placed.

Mr. W. Bennett Dawe, of Hill, near Ashburton, together with his family, saw one on several nights in succession in the autumn of 1898. The month of September had been very hot and dry, and this was succeeded by a heavy rainfall in October during twenty-three days. The mean temperature of the month was 54·7, being 4° above the average of twenty years. The warm damp season following on the heated ground and the boggy deposits in the Dart valley resulted in the generation of a good deal of decomposition. Mr. Dawe and several of his household observed at night a light of a phosphorescent nature in the meadows between Ashburton and Pridhamsleigh. It appeared to hover a little above the ground and dance to and fro, then race off in another direction, as if affected by currents of air. This was watched during several evenings, and the members of his family were wont as darkness fell to go out and observe it. The meadows are on deep alluvial soil, formerly marsh, and were drained perhaps sixty years ago.

The same gentleman saw a similar flame in the form of a ball some forty years previously in the low and then marshy valley between Tor Abbey gateway and the Paignton road, near where is now the Devon Rosery. The valley was then undrained. The gas generated, which catches fire on rising to the surface, is phosphoretted hydrogen, and is certainly evolved by decay of animal matter in water; if occasionally seen in churchyards it is probably after continued rain, when the graves have become sodden.

Jack-o'-lantern is called in Yorkshire Peggy-wi'-t'-wisp; consequently the treacherous, misleading character is there attributed to a sprite of that sex which has misled man from the first moment she appeared on earth—who never rested till she had led him out of the terrestrial paradise into one of her own making.

I was talking about this one evening in a little tavern, over the fire, to a Cornishman, when he laughed and volunteered a song. It was one, he said, that was employed as a test to see whether a man were sober enough to be able to repeat the numbers correctly that followed at the close of each stanza.*

---

* I have had to considerably tone down the original, which was hardly presentable if given *verbatim*.

"As I trudged on at ten at night
  My way to fair York city,
I saw before a lantern light
  Borne by a damsel pretty.
I her accos't, 'My way I've lost,
  Your lantern let me carry!
Then through the land, both hand in hand,
  We'll travel. Prithee tarry.'

        20, 18, 16, 14, 12, 10, 8, 6, 4, 2,
        19, 17, 15, 13, 11, 9, 7, 5, 3, 1.

"She tripp'd along, so nimble she,
  The lantern still a-swinging,
And 'Follow, follow, follow me!'
  Continually was singing.
'Thy footsteps stay!' She answered, 'Nay!'
  'Your name? You take my fancy.'
She laughing said, nor turn'd her head,
  'I'm only Northern Nancy.'

            20, 18, 16, etc.

"She sped along, I in the lurch,
  A lost and panting stranger,
Till, lo! I found me at the Church,
  She'd led me out of danger.
'Ring up the clerk,' she said; 'yet hark!
  Methinks here comes the pass'n;
He'll make us one, then thou art done;
  He'll thee securely fasten.'

            20, 18, 16, etc.

"'Man is a lost and vagrant clown
  That should at once be pounded,'
She said, and laid the matter down
  With arguments well grounded.
For years a score, and even more,
  I've lain in wedlock's fetter,
Faith! she was right; here, tied up tight,
  I could not have fared better

            20, 18, 10, etc."

An industry on Dartmoor that has become completely extinct is the collection of lichen from the rocks for the use of the dyers. There exists in MS. an interesting book by a Dr. Tripe, of Ashburton, recording what he saw and did each day, at the close of last century. He says that he observed women scraping off the lichen from the rocks near the Drewsteignton cromlech. This they sold to the dyers, who dried it, reduced it to powder, and treated it with a solution of tin in *aqua fortis* and another ingredient, when a most vivid scarlet dye was produced. The lichen is called botanically *Lichinoides saxatile*. Other lichens were employed to give purple and yellow colours. The cudbear and crab's-eye lichens (*Lecanora tartarea* and *Lecanora parella*) gave a dye of a royal purple, and the two species called *Parmelia saxatilis* and *Parmelia omphalodes* gave a yellowish brown. Moss also was employed for the purpose; the *Hypnum cupressiforme* yielded a rich reddish brown.

"Lichens and mosses," says Mr. Parfitt, "are the pioneers of the vegetable kingdom in attacking the hard and almost impenetrable rocks, and so preparing the way for the more noble plants—the trees and shrubs—by gradual disintegration, and by adding their own dead bodies to the soil, enrich it for the food of others."*

It is marvellous to see how the lichen attaches itself to the granite. A harshly glaring piece that the quarrymen have cut is touched with fine specks that spread into black and crocus-yellow circles, and

* "The Lichen Flora of Devonshire," in *Transactions of the Devonshire Association*, 1883.

tone down the stone to a sober tint. Unhappily of
late years there has been much firing of the furze
and heather on the moor, and the flames destroy the
beautiful lichens and mosses, and leave the old stones
white and ghostly, not to be reclothed with the old
tints for centuries.

I do not think that we have any idea of the slow-
ness with which the lichens spread ; a century to
them is nothing—it passes as a watch in the night.
There is a granite post I often go by. It was set
up just seventy years ago, and on it the largest
golden circle of the *Physcia parietina* has attained
the diameter of an inch. Mr. Parfitt mentions in
connection with it a rocky crag at Baggy Point,
North Devon, where it covers the whole surface with
a coat of golden colour. It spreads more rapidly
on slate than it does on granite, and especially on
such slates as are liable to rapid disintegration. The
Woodland and the Coryton slates are readily attacked
by it. The growth begins with a splash about the
size of a sixpence, and increases to that of a plate,
when the centre breaks up, and the ring becomes
detached in fragments which meet others, and so
appear to cover the rock or roof.

One of the most beautiful of the lichens on the
moor is the coral moss, *Sphærophoron coralloides*. It
is a pale greenish-white, upright-growing lichen, that
forms a cup, and somewhat resembles an old Venetian
wineglass. Then points of brilliant scarlet form
round the lip of the cup, and increase in size till
the whole presents a wonderful appearance as of
sealing-wax splashed over the soil. It is not con-

fined to the moorland, but grows also in woods,
where there has been a clearance made.   I came
upon a wonderful carpet of sprinkled scarlet and
white on one occasion, where there was a woodman's
track through an old oak coppice.   But it must be
capricious, for of late years when searching for it in
the same spot I have found no more.   The black
coral moss is scarce, but it has been found about
Lynx and Yes Tors.

The birds on Dartmoor have a hard time of it, not
only because of the guns levelled at them, but because
of the "swaling" or burning of the moor, which takes
place at the time when they are nesting.   In East
Anglia there are along the coast the "bird tides,"
as the people say.   At that period when the plovers
and sea-mews are nesting in the marshes, there are un-
usually low tides, a provision of God, so it is held, for
the protection of the feathered creatures whilst laying
and hatching out their eggs.   So the ancients told of
the halcyon days when the gods had pity on the sea-
birds, and smoothed seven to eleven days in the winter
solstice, that they might with safety hatch their young.
But on Dartmoor man has none of this pity ; he
selects the very time when the poor birds are sitting
in their nests on their eggs, or are cherishing their
callow young, for enveloping them in flames.   The
buzzard, the hen-harrier, and the sparrow-hawk are
now chiefly seen in the most lonely portions of the
moor.   Gulls visit it on the approach of stormy
weather ; but the ring-ouzel is there throughout the
year.   The golden and grey plovers are abundant ;
the pipe of the curlew may be heard ; black grouse

and quail may be shot, as also snipe. By the water, that living jewel the kingfisher can be observed watching for his prey, and about every farm the blue tit, called locally the hicky maul or hicka noddy, is abundant. The sand martin breeds in a few places. The heron has a place where she builds at Archerton.

The snow bunting and cirl bunting are met with occasionally.

The cuckoo is heard on the moor before he visits the lowlands. "March, he sits on his perch; April, he tunes his bill; May, he sings all day; June, he alters his tune, and July, away he do fly." So say the people.

One of the freshest and most delicious of Devonshire folk-melodies is that connected with a song about the cuckoo.

> "The cuckoo is a pretty bird,
>   She sings as she flies ;
> She bringeth good tidings,
>   She telleth no lies.
> She sucketh sweet flowers
>   To keep her voice clear,
> And when she sings 'Cuckoo'
>   The summer draweth near." *

There is a saying among the country folk :—

> " Kill a robin or a wren,
>   Never prosper, boy or man."

The wren is said to·be the king of all birds. The story told to account for this is that the birds once assembled to elect a sovereign, and agreed that that

---

* Given in *A Garland of Country Song.*   Methuen, 1895.

one of the feathered creation who soared highest should be esteemed king. The eagle mounted, and towered aloft high above the rest, but was outwitted by the wren, who, unobserved and unfelt, had hopped on to the eagle's back.

The birds were so distressed and angry at the trick that they resolved to drown the wren in their tears. Accordingly they procured a pan into which each bird in turn wept. When it was nearly full the blundering old owl came up. "With such big eyes," said the birds, "he will weep great tears." But he perched on the edge of the pan and upset it. Thenceforth the wren has reigned undisputed king of the birds.

There is a curious story told of a wren. In one of the Irish rebellions a party of British military were out after the enemy when, having made a long march, they lay down to sleep and left no one to keep sentinel. As they lay slumbering the murderous rascals stole up, creeping like snakes in the grass and among the bushes, and would have butchered the entire party had it not been for a wren, which, perching on the drum belonging to the company, tapped it repeatedly with its little beak. This roused the soldiers, they became aware of their situation, and were able just in time to fire on their assailants and disperse them.

In Ireland, and in Pembrokeshire and elsewhere in South Wales, it was usual, on S. Stephen's Day or at the New Year, to put a wren in a lantern that was decorated with ribbons and carry it about to farms and cottages, with a song, which was repaid by a small coin. Whether such a custom existed in Devon I cannot say; I remember nothing of the sort.

The sparrow-hawk is often seen quivering aloft in the air. A curious story is told of one by Mr. Elliot.

"As is well known, not only sparrow-hawks, but other birds of prey as well as other species, repair to the same site year after year for nesting. This knowledge is valuable to the keepers, who look up these haunts and try to shoot the old birds before they hatch their eggs. On one occasion he shot the female as she came off the nest, and this satisfied him, but on visiting the spot later he was surprised at another female flying off; on climbing to the nest he found that the male must have found another mate, as they had built a second nest over and into the old one, which contained four eggs, whilst the freshly-built nest contained five." *

One has supposed hitherto that the gay widower who looked out for another spouse after having lost the first was a product of the human species only.

A visitor to Dartmoor in June or July will be surprised to find flights of rooks over it. As soon as their maternal cares are over, they desert the rookeries on the lowland and go for change of air and diet to the moor, where they feed on the whortleberry, possibly, but most certainly on the daddy longlegs and its first cousin, who is the hateful wireworm in his fully developed form. A friend one day saw a bit of the moor dense with rooks,

* E. A. S. Elliot, "Birds in the South Hams," *Transactions of the Devonshire Association,* 1899

and surprised at their movements and excitement, observed them closely, and discovered that they were having a glut of daddy longlegs. The light and friable peat earth exactly suits the wireworm in its early stages, and when the pest emerged from the soil full blown, then the rooks were down on him before he could come to our gardens and turnip fields to devastate them.

The one deficiency in the soil on Dartmoor is lime. That will sweeten the grass and enable the cattle to thrive. Bullocks and other cattle will do on the moor, but they really need a change to land on lime whilst they are growing. The roots of the grass and heather are ravenous after lime, and for this reason it is that of the many interments on the moor hardly a particle of bone remains.

From Post Bridge starts the Lych Way, the Road of the Dead, along which corpses were conveyed to Lydford, the parish church, until, in 1260, Bishop Bronescombe gave licence to the inhabitants of Dartmoor, who lived nearer to Widdecombe than to Lydford, to resort thither for baptisms and funerals.

The Lych Way may be traced from Conies Down Tor to Whitabarrow; thence it strikes for Hill Bridge, and so across the spur of Black Down to Lydford church.

When I was a boy I heard strange tales of the Lych Way—and of funerals being seen passing over it of moonlight nights. But superstition is dead now on Dartmoor, as elsewhere, and ghosts as well as pixies have been banished, not as the old moormen say, by the "ding-dongs" of the church and mission chapel bells, but by the voice of the schoolmaster.

A walk or scramble down the Dart will take to the ruins of the Snaily House, the story concerning which I have told elsewhere.* It may be carried on to Dartmeet, where a little colony of inhabitants will be found, and a return may be taken over Bellever Tor, a striking height that holds its own, and seems to be the true centre of the moor. On its slopes are several kistvaens, but all have been robbed of their covering-stones. There is an unpleasant morass between Bellever Tor and the highroad.

I was witness here of a rather amusing scene. A gentleman with his wife and a young lady friend of hers had driven out, from Princetown or Tavistock, and when near Bellever the latter expressed a wish to go to the summit of the tor. The gentleman looked at his better half, who gave consent with a nod, whereupon he started with the young lady, and his wife drove on and put up the horse at Post Bridge, then walked back to meet the two as they returned to the high-road, on which madame promenaded. Now, as it fell out, the husband missed his way on trying to reach the high-road, and got to the morass, where he and the young lady walked up and down, and every now and then he extended his hand and helped her along from one tuft of grass to another. They went up—got more involved—then down again, and were fully half an hour in the morass.

* *Dartmoor Idylls.* Methuen, 1896.

Madame paced up and down the road, glaring at her husband and the young lady dallying on the moor, as she took it; for she was quite unable to apprehend the reason why they did not come to her as the crow flies, and as she considered was her due. Her pace was accelerated, her turns sharper, her glances more indignant, as minute after minute passed. She saw them approach, then turn and retrace their steps, gyrate, holding each other's hands, and walk down the slope some way. Then along the road, snorting like a war-horse, went the lady. She flourished her parasol at them; she called, they paid no attention. Finally they headed the swamp and arrived on the firm road. Thereupon the lady strode forward speechless with wrath towards Post Bridge and the inn, where a high tea was ready. Not a word would she vouchsafe to either. Not a word of explanation would she listen to from her husband.

Curious to see the end, I went on to Webb's Inn, and came in on the party.

The gentleman sat limp and crestfallen.

An excellent tea was ready. Cold chicken, ham, whortleberry jam and Devonshire cream. He ate nothing.

" My dear," said madame to her husband, "you are not eating."

" No, precious ! " he replied.   " I have lost my appetite."

" But," retorted she, " the moor gives one."

" Not to me," he responded feebly.   " I don't feel well.   The moor has taken mine away."

s

Obviously there had been an interview, *tête-à-tête*, before they sat down.

Presently I saw them drive away.

Madame brandished the whip and held the reins, and the young lady friend sat in front.

Monsieur was behind, disconsolate and sniffing.

CHAPTER XVII.

PRINCETOWN

KING LOUIS XIV. selected the most barren
and intractable bit of land out of which to
create Versailles, with its gardens, plantations, and
palace; and Sir Thomas Tyrwhitt chose the most
inhospitable site for the planting of a town. Sir
Thomas was Black Rod, and Warden of the Stannaries. He was a man of a sanguine temperament,
for he calculated on reaping gold where he sowed
shillings, and that in Dartmoor bogs.

At his recommendation prisons were erected at
Princetown in 1806, at a cost of £130,000, for the
captives in the French and American wars. Sir
George Magrath, M.D., the physician who presided
over the medical department from 1814 until the
close of the war, testified to the salubrity of the
establishment.

"From personal correspondence with other establish-
ments similar to Dartmoor, I presume the statistical record
of that great tomb of the living (embosomed as it is in

a desert and desolate waste of wild, and in the winter time terrible scenery, exhibiting the sublimity and grandeur occasionally of elemental strife, but never partaking of the beautiful of Nature ; its climate, too, cheerless and hyperborean), with all its disadvantages, will show that the health of its incarcerated tenants, in a general way, equalled, if not surpassed, any war prison in England or Scotland. This might be considered an anomaly in sanitary history, when we reflect how ungenially it might be supposed to act on southern constitutions ; for it was not unusual in the months of December and January for the thermometer to stand at thirty-three to thirty-five degrees below freezing, indicating cold almost too intense to support animal life. But the density of the congregated numbers in the prison created an artificial climate, which counteracted the tor-pifying effect of the Russian climate without. Like most climates of extreme heat or cold, the new - comers re-quired a seasoning to assimilate their constitution to its peculiarities, in the progress of which indispositions, incidental to low temperature, assailed them ; and it was an everyday occurrence among the reprobate and incorrigible classes of the prisoners, who gambled away their clothing and rations, for individuals to be brought up to the receiving room in a state of suspended animation, from which they were usually resuscitated by the process resorted to in like circumstances in frigid regions. I believe one death only took place during my sojourn at Dartmoor, from torpor induced by cold, and the profligate part of the French were the only sufferers. As soon as the system became acclimated to the region in which they lived, health was seldom disturbed."

There were from seven to nine thousand prisoners incarcerated in the old portion of the establishment.

They were packed for the night in stages one above another, and we can well believe that by this means they " created an artificial climate," but it must have been an unsavoury as well as an unwholesome one.

Over the prison gates is the inscription " *Parcere subjectis*," and the discomfort of so many being crammed into insufficient quarters strikes us now, and renders the inscription ironical; but it was not so regarded or intended at the time. Our convicts are nursed in the lap of luxury as compared with the condition of the prisoners at the beginning of the century. But then the criminal is the spoiled child of the age, to be petted, and pampered, and excused.

A convict with one eye, his nose smashed on one side, with coarse fleshy lips, was accosted by the chaplain. "For what are you in here, my man?" "For bigamy," was the reply. " 'Twasn't my fault; the women would have me."

One marvels that such a deformed, plain spot as the *col* between the two Hessary Tors should have been selected for a town. The only reply one can give is that Sir Thomas Tyrwhitt and the Prince Regent would have it so. It is on the most inclement site that could have been selected, catching the clouds from the south-west, and condensing fog about it when everywhere else is clear. It is exposed equally to the north and east winds. It stands over fourteen hundred feet above the sea, above the sources of the Meavy, in the ugliest as well as least suitable situation that could have been selected; the site determined by Sir Thomas, so as to be near his granite quarries.

There have been various attempts made by prisoners to escape. One of the most desperate was in November, 1880, when a conspiracy had been organised among the convicts. At the time a good many were engaged in a granite quarry. They had agreed to make a sudden dash on the warders, overpower them, whilst in the quarry; and they chose for the attempt the day in the month on which the governor went to Plymouth to receive the money for payment of the officials, with intent to waylay, rob, and murder him, then to break up into parties of two, and disperse over the moor.

One of the conspirators betrayed them, so that the scheme was known. It was deemed advisable not in any way to alter the usual arrangements, lest this should inspire suspicion in the minds of the convicts. The warders, armed with rifles, who keep guard at a distance round the quarry, were told when they heard the chief warder's whistle to close round the quarry, and, if necessary, fire.

The gang was marched, as usual, under a slender escort, to the quarry, and work was begun as usual. All went well till suddenly the ringleader turned about and, with his crowbar, struck at the head warder and staggered him for the moment: he reeled and almost fell. Instantly the convict shouted to his fellows, "Follow me, boys! Hurrah for freedom!" And they made a dash for the entrance to the quarry.

Meanwhile the head warder had rallied sufficiently to whistle, but before the outer ring of guards appeared some of the under warders discharged their rifles at the two leading convicts. One fell dead, the other was riddled with shot, yet, strange to say, lived, and, I believe, is alive still.

Before the rest of the conspirators could master the warders in the quarry and get away, the men who had been summoned appeared on the edge of the hollow, that was like a crater, with their rifles aimed at the convicts, who saw the game was up, and submitted.

There are always some crooked minds and perverse spirits in England ready to side with the enemies of their country or of society, whether Boers or burglars; and so it was in this case. A great outcry was made at the shooting of the two ringleaders. If a warder had been killed, no pity would have been felt for him by these faddists. All their feelings of sympathy were enlisted on behalf of the wrongdoer.

A curious case occurred in 1895.

On March 10th, Sunday, at night, the chaplain, who lived in a house in the town, being unable to sleep, about half-past eleven went downstairs in his dressing-gown. He was surprised to notice a light approaching from the study. Then he observed a man emerge into the hall, holding a large clasp knife in his hand. On seeing the chaplain, whose name was Rickards, he uttered a yell, and rushed at him with the knife.

The chaplain, who maintained his nerve, said, " Stop this fooling, and come in here and let us have a little talk; you have clearly lost your way."

The fellow offered no resistance, and allowed himself to be led into the study, where the Rev. C.

Rickards quietly seated himself on the table, and said to the burglar, "Now, we shall get on better if you give me up that knife." At the same time he took hold of the blade and attempted to gain possession of it. He had disengaged two of the man's fingers from it, when the fellow drew the knife away, thereby badly cutting the chaplain's hand. Mr. Rickards then jumped off the table, exclaiming, "This is not fair!"

"Look here," said the burglar, "I won't be took at no price," and flourished the knife defiantly. Noticing that the fellow's pockets bulged greatly, Mr. Rickards said, "You're not going out with my property," and closed with him, and endeavoured to put his hand into one of the pockets. The burglar resisted, and made for the door. Mr. Rickards now got near where his gun hung on the wall; he took it down, and clicked the hammer. The gun was not loaded. The burglar then blew out the candle he carried, and ran from the room. Mr. Rickards at once loaded his gun with cartridges, and followed the fellow into the passage. He still had his own candle alight. The man then bolted into the drawing-room, and endeavoured to open the window. The chaplain entered, and said, "Now bail up; up with your arms, or I shall fire."

Thereupon the burglar made a dash at him, head down, and the chaplain retreated, the man rushing after him. Mr. Rickards had no desire to fire, and as the fellow plunged past him, he struck at him with the gun, but missed him. The fellow then dashed through the doorway, and ran again into the study. The chaplain pursued him, and, standing in the doorway, said, "Now I have you. The gun is loaded, and I shall certainly fire if you come towards me."

The burglar stood for a moment eyeing him, and then made a leap at him with the uplifted knife; and Mr. Rickards fired at his legs. The man was hit, and staggered back against the mantelboard. The chaplain said, "Have you had enough?"

Again the fellow gathered himself up with raised knife to fall on him, when Mr. Rickards said coolly, "The other barrel is loaded, and I shall fire if you advance." The man, however, again came on, when the chaplain fired again, and hit the man in his right arm, and the knife fell. Mr. Rickards stooped, picked up the knife, closed it, and put it into his pocket. Then, thinking that there might be more than this one man engaged in the burglary, he reloaded his gun. The burglar now went down in a lump on the hearthrug, bleeding badly.

By this time the house was roused; the servants had taken alarm, and had sent for the warders, who arrived, and a doctor was summoned.

The fellow had been engaged in a good many robberies prior to this.

One night a couple of young convicts escaped, and obtained entrance into the doctor's house, where evidently a large supper party had been held, as the tables had not been cleared after the departure of the guests. Afterwards, when retaken, one of the men said:—

"Sir, it was just as though the doctor had made

ready, and was expecting us to supper. The table
was laid, and there were chickens and ham, tongue,
and cold meats, with puddings, cakes, and decanters
of wine, making our mouths fairly water. We ate
and ate as only two hungry convicts could eat after
the semi-starvation of prison diet. I could not look
at a bit more when I had finished. 'Try just a leetle
slice more of this ham,' said my chum. 'No, thank
you, Bill; I couldn't eat another mouthful to save my
life.' And so we left, and were caught on going out."

Soon after this the chaplain visited the fellow who
had been recaptured, and seeing him depressed and
in a very unhappy frame of mind, said to him, "Anything on your soul, man? Your conscience troubling
you?"

"Terrible," answered the convict; "I shall never
get over my self-reproach—not taking another slice
of ham."

An old man succeeded in getting away in a fog;
he ran as far as Ilsington before he was caught.

When brought back he was rather oddly attired,
and amongst other things carried a labourer's hoe.
This he employed vigorously when crossing fields,
if anyone came in sight. When captured a farmer
came to view him. "Why, drat it," he exclaimed,
"that's the man I saw hoeing Farmer Coaker's stubble
fields the other day. It struck me as something new
in farming, and I was going to ask him what there
was in it that he paid a labourer to hoe his stubbles."
This same convict, who was acquainted with the
neighbourhood, whilst temporarily at large paid a
visit to his wife one night. He asked her to let him

come into the house, telling who he was. "Not likely; you don't come in here. The policeman's about the place, and I don't want 'ee," was her cheering reply.

During another recent escape from Dartmoor an amusing incident occurred in a lonely lane on a dark night in the neighbourhood of Walkhampton. Two warders on guard mistook an inoffensive but partially inebriated farmer for the escaped convict, and he mistook them for a couple of runaways.

"Here he comes," exclaimed one warder to the other at the sound of approaching footsteps. "Now for him," as they both pounced out of the hedge where they had been in hiding, and seized hold of the man.

"Look here, my good fellows," he cried. "I know who you be. You be them two runaways from Princetown, and I'll give you all I've got, clothes and all, if only you won't murder me. I've got a wife and childer to home. I'm sure now I don't a bit mind goin' home wi'out any of my clothes on to my body. My wife'll forgive that, under the sarcumstances; but to go back wi'out nother my clothes nor my body either—that would be more nor my missus could bear and forgive. I'd niver hear the end of it."

Formerly the manner in which escapes were made was by the convicts when peat-cutting building up a comrade in a peat-stack, but the warders are now too much on the alert for this to take place successfully.

Such buildings as have been erected at Princetown are ugly. The only structure that is not so is the

"Plume of Feathers," erected by the French prisoners. Every other house is hideous, and most hideous of all are the rows of residences recently erected for the warders, for they are pretentious as well as ugly.

Yet Princetown may serve as a centre for excursions, if the visitor can endure the intermittent rushes of the trippers on their "cherry-bangs," and the persistent presence of the convict. If he objects to these, he can find accommodation a couple of miles off, at Two Bridges; but if he desire creature comforts he is sure of good entertainment at Princetown.

The group of remains at Merrivale Bridge is within an easy walk. These are the most famous on Dartmoor—not for their size or consequence, but because most accessible, being beside the road. But the whole collection is happily very complete.

There is a menhir, a so-called sacred circle, stone rows, a kistvaen, a pound, hut circles, and a cairn.

The menhir was the starting-point of a stone row that has been plundered for the construction of a wall. The sacred circle is composed of very small stones, and probably at one time inclosed a cairn. The stone rows that exist are fairly perfect. Those on the south, a double row, start from a cairn at the west end that has been almost destroyed, and end in blocking-stones to the east. They are, however, interrupted by a small cairn within a ring of stones, and, curiously enough, much as at Chagford, another row starts near it at a tangent from a partly destroyed cairn. The double row runs 849 feet.

The north pair of rows is imperfect; it probably had a cairn at the west end, but of it no traces now

STAPLE TOR

remain. It consists of a double row, and ends in a blocking-stone at the east end. It can be traced for only 590 feet.

A fine kistvaen, formerly in a cairn, lies to the south of the southern pair of rows. A few years ago a stonecutter at Merrivale Bridge took a gatepost out of the coverer. In this kistvaen have been found, though previously rifled, a flint knife and a polishing stone. There were formerly two large cairns near, but both have been destroyed by the road-makers, as have also many of the hut circles; a good many, however, yet remain, and some are inclosed within a pound. In this ground is an apple-crusher, like an upper millstone, that has been cut, but never removed, because the demand for these stones ceased with the introduction of the screw-press. Some ardent but not experienced antiquaries have supposed it to be a cromlech! As such it is figured in Major Hamilton Smith's plan of the remains in 1828.

The tor Over Tor, on the right-hand side of the road, was overthrown by some trippers—the first swallows of a coming flight—early in the century.

The descent to Merrivale Bridge is fine; the bold tors of Roos and Staple stand up grandly above the Walkham river. Walkham, by the way, is Walla-combe, the valley of the Walla.

The flank of Mis Tor towards the river is strewn with inclosures and hut circles.

On Staple Tor is a so-called tolmen, a freak of nature, unassisted by art. Cox Tor beyond is crowned with cairns, but they have been rifled.

A very charming excursion may be made by

following the Plymouth road to Peak Hill, then descending to Hockworthy Bridge, and ascending the river as best possible thence, by Woodtown to Merrivale Bridge. There is a lane above Ward Bridge that mounts the hillside on the east, and commands a fine view of Vixen Tor with Staple and Roos Tors behind. In the evening, when the valley is in purple shade, a flood of golden glory from the west illumines Vixen Tor, and this is the true light in which the river should be ascended. A so-called cyclopean bridge is passed that spans a stream foaming down to join the Walkham.

Walkhampton church need not arrest the pedestrian; it has a fine tower, but contains absolutely nothing of interest. Adjoining the churchyard is, however, a very early church house, probably more ancient than the present Perpendicular church.

Sampford Spiney has its village church, a quaint, small, old manor house, and a good tower to the church. It is somewhat curious that the dedication of neither of these churches is recorded.

Within an easy stroll of Princetown to the south is Harter Tor. There are here many hut circles, and below Harter Tor are stone avenues leading from cairns.

Black Tor, that looks down on these remains, is also above a blowing-house and miners' hut, not of an ancient date, as it had a chimney and fireplace. The mould-stone lies in the grass and weed.

Black Tor has on it a logan stone that can be rocked by taking hold of a natural handle. On its summit is a rock basin.

OLD BLOWING-HOUSE ON THE MEAVY

Tor Royal was built by Sir Thomas Tyrwhitt, and there he entertained the Prince Regent when that worthy visited Dartmoor. Tradition tells of high revelry and debauches taking place on that occasion. Sir Thomas planted trees that are doing fairly well.

BLOWING-HOUSE BELOW BLACK TOR.

In the valley of the West Dart, under Longaford and Littaford Tors, is Wistman's Wood, now sadly reduced in size. It has been assumed to be the last remains of the forest that once covered Dartmoor. But no forest ever did that; at all events no forest of trees. The ashes of the fires used by the primitive inhabitants show that peat was their principal fuel, and that what oak and alder they burned was small and stunted.

In the sheltered combes doubtless trees grew, but not to any height and size.

The early antiquaries, S. Rowe and E. Atkyns Bray, talked much tall nonsense about Wistman's Wood as a sacred grove, dedicated to the rites of Druidism, and of the collection of mistletoe from the boughs of the oaks. As it happens, there are no prehistoric monuments near the wood to indicate that it was held in reverence, and no mistletoe grows in Devon, and in Somersetshire only on apple trees. Indeed, the mistletoe will not grow higher than five or six hundred feet above the sea, and Wistman's Wood is not much less than a thousand feet above the sea-level.

In July, 1882, the central portion of the wood was set fire to, it was thought by trippers, in an attempt to boil a kettle. This has helped to reduce the ancient wood; but what prevents its increase is the sheep, which eat the young trees as they shoot up. It has been said that Wistman's Wood oaks produce no acorns. This, however, is not the case. The trees are so venerable that their power to bear fruit is nearly over, yet they still produce some acorns, and there are young oaks growing—but not where sheep roam—that have come from these parent stocks.

By ascending Bairdown, aiming for Lydford Tor, and then following the ridge almost due north, but with a little deflection to the west, Devil Tor may be reached, and near this stands the most impressive menhir on the moor, the Bairdown Man. The height is only twelve feet, but it is clothed in black lichen, and stands in such a solitary spot that it inevitably leaves an impression on the imagination. There is no token of there having ever been a stone row in connection with it.

It may here be noticed that the names Lydford Tor, Littaford, Longaford, Belleford, Reddaford, do not apply to any *fords* over the streams, which may be crossed without difficulty, but take their appellation from the Celtic *fordd*, "a way," and the tors about the Cowsick and West Dart take their titles from the great central causeway or from the Lych Way that passed by them.

The portion of the Cowsick above Two Bridges abounds in charming studies of river, rock, and timber.

An excursion to Great Mis Tor will enable the visitor to see a large rock basin, the Devil's Frying-pan as it is called, and then, if he descends Greena-ball, where are cairns, he will see on the slope opposite him, beyond the Walkham, a large village, consisting of circular pounds and hut circles. On reaching the summit of the hill he will see a fine circle of upright stones. It was originally double, but nearly all the stones forming the outer ring have been removed. The rest were fallen, but have been re-erected by His Grace the Duke of Bedford.

In such a case there can be no arbitrary restoration, for the holes that served as sockets for the stones can always be found, together with the trigger-stones. Indeed, it is easy by the shape of the

T

socket-holes to see in which way the existing stones were planted.

About half a mile to the north-west is the Langstone, which gives its name to this down; it is of a basaltic rock, and not, as is usual, of granite. Fice's Well, which I remember in the midst of moor, is now included within the newtake of the prisons, and a wall has been erected to protect it. This deprives it of much of its charm. It was erected by John Fitz in 1568. Cut on the granite coverer are the initials of John Fitz and the date.

The tradition is that John Fitz of Fitzford and his lady were once pixy-led whilst on Dartmoor. After long wandering in vain effort to find their way, they dismounted to rest their horses by a pure spring that bubbled up on a heathery hillside. There they quenched their thirst; but the water did more than that—it opened their eyes, and dispelled the pixy glamour that had been cast over them, so that at once they were able to take a right direction so as to reach Tavistock before dark night fell. In gratitude for this, John Fitz adorned the spring with a granite structure, on which were cut in low-relief his initials and the date of his adventure.

There are some old crosses that may be seen by such as are interested in these venerable relics. The Windy-post stands between Barn Hill and Feather Tor, and there are also two on Whitchurch Down. One of these, the more modern, of the fifteenth century, has lost its shaft, and is reduced to a head; but the other cross may, perhaps, date from the seventh century—it may even be earlier. Whitchurch was an archpriesthood; there were two of these in Devon and one in Cornwall. The origin of these archpriesthoods is probably this.

In Celtic countries the king liked to have his household priest, who ministered to the retinue and to his family. On the other hand, the tribe had its own saint, who was the ecclesiastical official for the tribe and educated the young.

As the kings increased in power, and the old tribal arrangement broke down, they had their household priests consecrated bishops, and the tribal lands were constituted their dioceses. But in Devon and Cornwall this could not be, as the Saxons took all power away from the native princes, and the Latin ecclesiastics would not endure the peculiar ecclesiastical organisation of the Celts. The household priests of the conquered chieftains therefore simply remained as archpriests. The Saxon and then the Norman nobles were not averse from having their own chaplains free from episcopal jurisdiction, and in some places the archpriest remained on. But the bishops did not like them, and one by one gobbled them up. Whitchurch was regulated by Bishop Stapeldon in 1332. At present only one archpriesthood lingers on, that of Haccombe. At an episcopal visitation, when the name of the archpriest is recited by the episcopal official, he does not respond, as to answer the citation would be a recognition of the bishop's jurisdiction over Haccombe. The very fine piece of screen in Whitchurch was placed there by a former Lord Devon. It comes from Moreton Hampstead. When the dunderheads there cast it forth, the Earl secured it and placed it where it might be preserved and valued. It is of excellent work.

Before laying down my pen I feel that I have not done homage to that which, after all, gives the flavour of poetry to the moorland—the heath and heather. I was one day on the top of the coach from Holsworthy to Bude, between two Scotch ladies, and I put to them the question, "Which is heath and which heather—that with the large, or that with the small bells?" And Jennie, on my right, said: "The large bell—that is heather"; but Grizel, on my left, said: "Nay, the small bell—that is heather." As Scottish women were undecided, I referred to books, and take their decision. The large bell is heath; the ling, that is heather.

In old times, so it is said, the Picts made of the heather a most excellent beer, and the secret was preserved among them. Leyden says that when the Picts were exterminated, a father and son, who alone survived, were brought before Kenneth the Conqueror, who promised them life if they would divulge the secret of heather ale. As they remained silent, the son was put to death before the eyes of his father. This exercise of cruelty failed in its effect. "Sire," said the old Pict, "your threats might have influenced my son, but they have no effect on me." The king suffered the Pict to live, and the secret remained untold.

Ah, weel! the Scotch make up for their loss upon whisky.

A recent writer, referring to the story, says: "It is just possible that the grain of truth contained in the tradition may be, that all the northern nations, as the Swedes still do, used the narcotic gale (*Myrica gale*), which grows among the heather, to give bitterness and strength to the barley beer ; and hence the belief that the beer was made chiefly of the heather itself."

I do not hold this. I suspect that the ale was metheglin, made of the honey extracted from the heather by the bees. Metheglin is still made round Dartmoor, but it is only good and "heady" when many years old. Avoid that which is younger than three winters. When it is older, drink sparingly.*

It is quite certain that the ancient Irish brewed a beer, which we can hardly think came from barley. S. Bridget has left but one poetical composition behind her, and that begins :—

> "I should like a great lake of ale
> For the King of kings.
> I should like the whole company of Heaven
> To be drinking it eternally !"

The heath was doubtless largely used in former times, from the Prehistoric Age, not only as a thatch for the huts and hovels, but as a litter for the beds. Indeed, heath or heather is still employed in the Scottish Highlands along with the peat earth as a substitute for mortar between the stones of which a cottage is built. And that heather was employed for bedding who can question? Leather is tanned

---

* Yet there is the Devonshire white ale—the composition of which is a secret—that is still drunk in the South Hams, and in one tavern in Tavistock. It is a singular, curdy liquor, in the manufacture of which egg is employed. Is heath used also? *Qu en sabe ?*

even better with heath than with oak-bark, and of it a brilliant yellow dye is produced.

But—ah, me! the heath and the heather!—it is not for the beer produced therefrom, not for the tan, not for the dye, that we love it. Wonderful is the sight of the moorside flushed with pink when the heather is in bloom—it is as though, like a maiden, it had suddenly awoke to the knowledge that it was lovely, and blushed with surprise and pleasure at the discovery.

But how shortlived is the heath!

It lies dead—a warm chocolate-brown, mantling the hills from October till July. Only in the midsummer does it timidly put forth its leaves—its spines rather—and then it flushes again in September. It blooms for about a fortnight, perhaps three weeks, and then subsides into its brown winter sleep. But what browns! what splendours of colour we have when the fern is in its russet decay and the heather is in its velvet sleep!

To him who wanders over the moor, and looks at the flowers at his feet, some day comes the proud felicity of lighting on the white heath—and that found ensures happiness. And I, as I make my *congé*, hand it to my reader with best wishes for his enjoyment of that region I love best in the world.

INDEX

279